Black Theology,
Black Power &
Black Love

by Minister Michael James

D1206829

Front Cover Illustration by Angelou Williams

First Edition

First Printing

Copyright © 2000 by Michael James

Contents

Acknowledgments

It is only proper and fitting that I salute the academic achievements and philosophies of Dr. James H. Cone, Dr. Martin L. King, Jr., and Malcolm X. Combined, their legacies form the foundation upon which my idea of a new African American Liberation Theology evolved. I am in their debt.

Many thanks to Dr. Dennis Groh, Dr. Rosemary Reuther, Dr. Larry Murphy, and Dr. Rosemary Keller—the staff of the history department at Garrett Evangelical Theological Seminary. Their counsel was invaluable. The unique teaching style of Mrs. Elisa Denja, a friend and Loyola University professor, opened the doors of my mind. She created within me an insatiable thirst to achieve a high standard of excellence in my academic pursuits.

With Sarra Shkolnik's encouragement and tutoring, I was able to complete my undergraduate studies and secure entry into graduate school. Thank you, Sarra, for your support. Kathy Hickman, a friend sent by God, never doubted my character or abilities. My love for her will never die. Tom Betten believed in my ability to write and stood with me during press conferences, protests, and marches in some of the most violent communities in Chicago. Derrick Ewing, a friend who became my brother, inspires me with his ability to overcome tremendous obstacles. Jonathan Walker, a God appointed mentor who entered my life at a very crucial state—he can be considered nothing less than my personal hero and a positive role model for African American males.

For steering me to the Lord, many thanks to Rev. Robert Thomas, a special brother in Christ. The powerful prayers of Rev. Tim Johnson helped me when I was down. Truman Rogers has defined for me the meaning of friendship: he stands by my side anywhere, anytime, and by any means necessary—no questions asked. Danny Wilson is a gifted brother who, one day, will be recognized for his special anointing of music. His messages in music continue to inspire me.

Praise the Lord for my children, my gifts from God: Octavious, Renisha, and Sariese. I give enormous thanks and applause to my oldest brother, George Frank James. Although George died shortly after the Vietnam War, his influence is still with me today. He was a brother, friend, and surrogate father who saved me from drugs, crime, and gangs. His convictions, encouragement; and love played a major role in my personal and educational development.

Last but not least, many thanks to my oldest sister Elizabeth (Penny) Veal for her unselfish encouragement during the dark years of my life. It was her persistence, prayers, and love that steered me back to the Lord.

To the memory of my oldest brother and sister, George F. James and Elizabeth (Penny) Veal. Because of you

The Message Continues...

Introduction

How is it that a poor African American boy whose family migrated from Greenwood, Mississippi, during the latter part of the Great Migration was called by the Lord to develop the next evolutionary step in Black Liberation Theology, a new African American Liberation Theology? F.A.I.T.H. (Forsaking All I Trust Him) best explains it.

I can still vividly remember the segregated ride to Chicago on the Greyhound bus, a foreshadowing of things to come in the most segregated city in the nation. I was raised on the West Side of Chicago (Lawndale area). We were a close-knit community, but poor. Hard hit by high rates of unemployment, racial discrimination, and welfare dependency, our families began to splinter. As a result, Lawndale, like most urban communities, succumbed to crime, violence, drugs, and gang activity. Without an early introduction to Almighty God and a sound Christian upbringing, I would not have defeated the shackles of poverty, welfare, and hopelessness.

It was during the 1960s that I began to see a glimmer of hope in the activities and scholarship of three special men: Dr. Martin L. King, Jr., Malcolm X, and Dr. James Cone. These men ignited a fire within my soul. Their courage was the catalyst that ultimately compelled me to conduct in-depth research into African American religious history. Although faced with insurmountable opposition, these noble pioneers boldly fought for liberation. As prophets, they demanded a change in the American values that perpetuated prejudice and discrimination against African Americans. As counselors, they sought to uplift the consciousness of Black people. As priests, they taught us about a Black Messiah who understood our predicament, shared our sorrows, and promised to deliver us from bondage.

History has depicted King, Malcolm X, and Cone as diametrically opposed in thought, word, deed, and philosophy. While there are aspects of their beliefs that appear to be irreconcilable, it is also true that they shared critical areas of common ground. Most important, they were unified in their goal of freedom for Black people. If we are to heal, we must reconcile the contributions of these great thinkers in our new strategies, political platforms, social theories and programs, theologies, and ministries. We must unify around their legacies and vision for us.

African American Liberation Theology (the Theology) synthesizes the philosophies of King, Malcolm X, and Cone around the issues of integration, separation, and nationalism. I believe the Theology has the power to heal the polarization between King's and Malcolm's philosophies in particular. The goal of this spiritual-social synthesis is a new consciousness in which we can finally begin to see ourselves as God's beloved community, delivered from all forms of bondage, and blessed, not cursed, by our Blackness. Racial, economic, political, and social equality can be achieved with the Theology as our foundation. The Theology is God's answer to our historical cry for liberation from the tentacles of White oppression.

It is only proper and fitting that I acknowledge the contributions of these three spiritual giants. We will explore the uniqueness of each man in the following chapters, but if they shared one common idea it was the powerful belief that Black people were chosen by God for a special purpose. For a people conditioned on a Christian theology designed to create and maintain a Black slavocracy, this was a revolutionary idea and it had the effect of stirring the Sleeping Giant. Slowly but surely, Black people began to awaken. African American Liberation Theology is my attempt to open our eyes even more.

Although African Americans were brought to this country in chains, we can no longer afford to behave like a defeated people. Our theology must serve us in that it opens our eyes to the God of love, mercy, compassion, and power, to a God that is on the side of the oppressed and victimized. Although we still face discrimination and prejudice, God is on our side. God has always been on our side, even during our darkest hours. This is a powerful statement of fact.

Who are we as African Americans? How are forces, both spiritual and carnal, shaping our history as a chosen people? Throughout our history God's crusades have shaped and molded us. He has used coercion, grace, and merciful influence to change us and our oppressors. We may not understand God's vision for us, but we must have faith in the process. One of the beliefs that has enabled Black people to survive is that all things (including evil intent) work together for the good of those who love the Lord and reverence His sovereign power.

Do not doubt that we are moving forward. We are progressing socially, psychologically, communally, and spiritually. Since emancipation, we have steadily evolved and we must give thanks to God for the unleashing of His spirit in our lives. From polytheism to monotheism, from slavery to Reconstruction to civil rights, we can track God's movement in our history, developing us into a people that will worship, serve, and co-create with Him.

Standing on the shoulders of Cone, King, and Malcolm, I have developed what I believe is the next evolutionary step in a theology designed to liberate Black people from the residue of victimization, dependency, suffering, and self-hatred that still lingers among and within us. African American Liberation Theology was written for ministers, lay workers, and all African Americans seeking salvation and deliverance from spiritual, personal, and social bondage.

In Part I, I examine the theologies and philosophies of King, Malcolm, and Cone that are relevant to the new African American Liberation Theology.

In Part II, I plumb the depths of the Old and New Testaments for their liberation messages. I define the new theology and lay a framework that will provide direction for pastors and the Black church to develop ministries that will meet the needs of Black people today.

Encompassed in this analysis, is the theological framework to the spiritual, social, and personal realities of Black people today. I examine Black consciousness, Black love, and Black power in the light of the new theology. Without the power of deliverance, this new theology is just an impotent collection of words and ideas. With God's power, the theology can become a motivating force in our lives.

God is moving our race in a new direction. A new Black race is being forged. We are no longer slaves. We are no longer beggars. We are metamorphosing into a spiritual people, a God-directed people, a responsible people. Although we are not a monolithic community with the same political, social, and spiritual agendas, God is still moving through our individualities to attain a common goal. God has revealed to me His revelation for our people, and it is this: *We, the descendants of Africa who have been strategically placed in the United States, are being prepared to advocate for the liberation of all Third World peoples.* African American Liberation Theology will allow us to do this from a position of strength, power, and love.

The following is my definition of African American Liberation Theology:

A theological compromise and synthesis of the philosophies of Martin Luther King, Malcolm X, and James Cone; a spiritual synthesis which combines integration, separation, and nationalism with the idea of the beloved community; a fusion of traditional Christian beliefs with the reality of the Black experience.

African American Liberation Theology is not just an intellectual exercise. It is to be applied to the African American quest for racial, economic, and political parity in America. It is God's answer to our personal cry for liberation from the tentacles of White oppression in North America.

All scriptures are taken from the traditional Old King James Version.

PART I
The Fathers of Black Liberation Theology

Chapter 1: Martin Luther King, Jr.

Dr. King's philosophy originated from within the walls of the Black church. The theology and ministries of this same autonomous Black church served as a sociopolitical platform for civil rights.

On December 1, 1955, the voice of God was heard loudly and clearly as Rosa Parks, an attractive seamstress, boarded a Cleveland Avenue bus destined for downtown Montgomery, Alabama. Parks' tired feet and tired spirit were used by God to halt the tireless progression of racism, degradation, and dehumanization of African American people.[1] It is a story we enjoy telling over and over, to our children and to each other. When the White bus driver ordered Parks to surrender her seat to a White passenger, she refused. She stayed seated. Segregation had come face to face with God. As in the days of the slavocracy, the prayers of Black people disturbed the status quo. It took just one tired woman to launch a chain of events that would change the world. The prayers of the righteous do avail much, and when we prayed, God unleashed His spirit upon an unjust world.

Parks' action triggered the Montgomery bus boycott. On December 5, 1955, Coretta and Martin King witnessed a nearly 100 percent cooperative effort by Blacks to derail segregation. Said King, "He who passively accepts evil is as much involved in it as he who helps to perpetrate it. He who accepts evil without protesting against it is really cooperating with it."[2] The Negro's passive peace was often bought at too great a price.

Through prayer and much soul searching, King came to the conclusion that the protest against the atrocities of his fellow White brothers must be met courageously, with dignity and Christian love. This was the Negro's greatest challenge and responsibility. If successful, he believed historians would write, "There lived a great people—a black people—who injected new meaning and dignity into the veins of civilization."[3]

Shortly after Rosa Parks' trial, Ralph Abernathy, E.D. Nixon, and Rev. E.N. French (ministers of Hilliard Chapel A.M.E. Zion Church) organized a meeting. Not surprisingly, Rev. King was elected president of the new movement and all agreed that the Montgomery Improvement Association (M.I.A.) would be the official name. King delivered a moving speech to a standing-room-only crowd at Holy Street Church. Outside, some 4,000 people stood cheering. Shortly after this inaugural speech, more than 50,000 Negroes marched to God's drumbeat until the deteriorating walls of segregation came down. The bus integration order reached Montgomery on December 20. On December 21, 1956, God dethroned public segregation in Montgomery.[4] The Black church, the National Association for the Advancement of Colored People (NAACP), the Student Nonviolent Coordinating Committee (SNCC), the Southern Christian Leadership Conference (SCLC), the Congress of Racial Equality (CORE), as well as many non-black organizations, became the catalysts for social change.

Throughout the nation, Negroes began to systematically challenge the forces of evil. Donothingism, escapism, and standstillism were readily replaced with action and nonviolent confrontation. Demonstrations, sit-ins, boycotts, and local marches engineered by the Black church and civil rights organizations inevitably culminated in the Great Event, the historical March on Washington on August 28, 1963.

Martin's Philosophy

Three themes shaped the faith and theology of King: *justice, love,* and *hope,* all of which were defined in the light of Jesus' suffering and death on the cross. For King, the cross was proof of God's willingness to save, deliver, and restore broken humanity and broken communities in particular.[5] "Segregation was the most blatant expression of brokenness between human beings in America."[6] The cross represented the unequivocal answer of *no* to alienation and segregation (which King believed was evil), and *yes* to reconciliation and integration.

In King's theology, the cross represented not only reconciliation but suffering as well. This suffering defined the way for those who accepted Christ and were transformed by His power. In our quest for liberation, African Americans willingly carried the suffering cross. Through Christ's redemption, believers received a special vocation: to continue His work and to spread the Good News throughout the world. In America, Negroes received

Christ's calling. The prime directive of the civil rights movement was to confront evil, break down the walls of segregation, and create a beloved community shared by Whites and African Americans.[7]

The cross and suffering of Jesus Christ laid the foundation of King's commitment to using nonviolence to achieve Black liberation. Individuals and entire churches submitted to crucifixion during the civil rights movement. Like Christ, we were persecuted and crucified for our beliefs.[8]

King believed that crucifixion leads to the reward of resurrection. God would never allow evil to triumph over good; in numerous speeches, King proclaimed that unmerited suffering is redemptive.[9] Oppressed people must use the weapon of morality to achieve just ends. This approach to social change was very similar to ones used in Ghandi's India, Ghana, and other African nations.

After a trip to India, King formed a new strategy. He was "more convinced than ever before that nonviolent resistance is the most potent weapon available to oppressed people in their quest for social justice."[10] Since hate is contrary to God's nature and will, any effort to achieve liberation must be devoid of hate, anger, malice, or violence. Violence of any kind is derived from hate. It indicates a crisis in faith. The violent individual no longer believes that God, the Creator of the universe, can sustain a beloved community.

King believed that Negroes and Whites could live together in peace. He had faith that God would make this social miracle happen. Practically, coexistence *had* to occur because most Blacks were undoubtedly going to stay in America, the land of their birth.[11] Even though Blacks disagreed with King on many points, most believed that we should all try to get along and treat each other with basic respect. Our very existence was at stake; noncompliance inevitably meant that no one would be able to survive.[12]

At the heart of King's perspective on nonviolence was agape love. Agape is distinct from *eros* and *philia* in that the latter involve mutual affection while agape love is unconditional and emanates from God. Agape love is identical to Ghandi's satyagraha.

Agape love is the unconditional surrender to the ideal of redemption as exemplified by Jesus Christ. This surrender involves loving everyone, even individuals who lack the ability to return love and whose ways are distasteful. You love them because God loves them.[13]

Agape love was a critical component in King's goal of full integration for African Americans. Rejecting all programs that advocated separation of the races, King pushed to desegregate at all levels of human and institutional intercourse; this would be the first giant step toward his overall plan of full integration.[14]

When the goals of the civil rights movement evolved to encompass the just society, the beloved community, desegregation, and full integration, the development of a healthy relationship based on forgiveness, love, and understanding between African Americans and Whites became paramount. The solution to political domination, economic exploitation, and social degradation of Black people had to be based on love not hate, forgiveness not vengeance. The White majority (ruling class) and the Black minority (the oppressed) had to learn to live peacefully in America as brothers and sisters.[15] Despite what he saw every day of his life, King believed that hatred and violence had no place on God's earth or in a civilized society.

On April 23–25, 1957, King addressed a mixed audience of African Americans and White ministers at the Conference on Christian Faith and Human Relations in Nashville, Tennessee. He said that "America's great advances in technology and science have enabled us to develop the greatest system of production, carve highways through the stratosphere, and cure some of the most dreaded diseases known to man. However, the chief moral dilemma of this great nation still haunts us in the form of 'racial conflict.'"[16] The failure to create a nation of brotherhood plagues us today. We still have not learned how to respect the worth and value of all humans. We have yet to learn the basic art of loving our neighbors.

As a result, the Church faces a tremendous challenge. Its charge is to narrow the gap between what we believe and what we practice. It has a duty to serve as the moral guardian of society and God will hold it accountable. As King discovered, segregation snuffs out society's ability to love one another. The unity we share through Christ becomes weakened. This evil, polarizing force is unchristian.[17]

King's analysis of the unchristian nature of segregation was based on three views: first, segregation produces a state of inequality; second, the soul of both the segregator and the segregated are sacred; and third, segregation depersonalizes the segregated and destroys any bridge which would allow reconciliation.[18] In that Nashville address, King reminded the White ministers that they were citizens of two opposing worlds—eternity and the world of flesh. While today they answer to man, one day they would have to answer to God.

King and his American dream underwent several changes during the two major periods of his preoccupation with nonviolent integration. The first period began in December 1955 with the Montgomery bus boycott and came to a triumphant close with the passing of the Voting Rights Bill in August of 1965. The second began during autumn of 1965 when King addressed the intricate connection between militarism, racism, and poverty under the auspices of unfair policies orchestrated by the U.S. government.[19]

Despite his compromises, it is important to remember that King was adamantly opposed to segregation and that he viewed it as evil. The conflict between the opposing forces of segregation and integration was defined by the conflicts between good and evil, justice and injustice.[20] The oneness of humanity and divine love as prime directives of the civil rights movement was where he kept his focus.[21] Nonviolent protest, expressed through the power of love, became the only logical, rational means of achieving desegregation and achieving an acceptable level of justice.

King became involved with Ella Baker, Stanley Levison, and Bayard Rustin. Collectively this group called upon African American ministers throughout the Southern belt to meet in Atlanta from January 10–11, 1957, at historical Ebenezer Baptist Church to brainstorm on exactly what freedom meant and how to constructively struggle for this elusive prize.[22] On February 14, this same group founded the Southern Christian Leadership Conference (SCLC). Dr. King was appointed the first president of the new organization. His goals were to permanently destroy the inhumane disease of segregation and redeem the soul of America.[23] Through nonviolent confrontation, they would achieve their ultimate goal: full integration and the creation of the beloved community in which humans could peacefully coexist.

The urgent necessity of integrating African Americans into America's mainstream was a constant theme in King's speeches.[24] Integration and the American Dream were stressed in his *Message Delivered at the Prayer Pilgrimage.*

King also addressed many other issues. For example, he called for courageous, dedicated leaders to promote justice at all levels so that African Americans could fully achieve their ambitions. He urged the executive branch of the federal government to enforce the law and protect *all* citizens. He challenged President Eisenhower to appoint a Negro to all White cabinets (Secretary of Integration) and establish a new branch of government (Bureau of Negro Affairs). He urged President Kennedy to issue a Second Emancipation Proclamation that would outlaw all forms of racial discrimination.[25] King accused both the presiding President and Congress of acting against democratic principles. Northern liberals were summoned by King to choose sides on the issue of racial justice; he wouldn't permit them to straddle the fence. Although White churches were not singled out during his speeches, King believed that White ministers were called by God to fight segregation.[26] He admonished the African American community to pursue five objectives: self-respect, high moral standards, whole-hearted work, leadership, and nonviolence.[27] Finally, to those who claimed that morality could not be given legislated, King argued that desegregation *could* be legislation.[28]

As a mediator, King developed the hypothesis that, "Men often hate each other because they fear each other; they fear each other because they do not know each other; they do not know each other because they cannot communicate; they cannot communicate because they are separated."[29]

Of course, nonviolence was the strategy for which Dr. King is remembered. For King, nonviolence was the offensive weapon that armed the battle for full integration. Nonviolence was the defensive strength that disarmed the oppressor by weakening morale, exposing weaknesses, and affecting the American conscience. Most importantly, nonviolence produced within the oppressed the courage to die if necessary.[30]

Chapter 2: Malcolm X

Malcolm X, a Muslim and follower of Elijah Muhammad, respected Dr. King for his efforts to liberate African American people, however, he wholeheartedly rejected the strategy of nonviolent confrontation. Malcolm believed God (Allah) gave Blacks the right to defend themselves against racism and violence. He often said that to respond to violence with nonviolence made no sense. Malcolm called King's nonviolence strategy unmanly and passive.[1] An eye for an eye was an ideal whose time had come!

This drum major for justice told his followers that God (Allah) had summoned the Black race from the shadows of enslavement and degradation. However, by no means did he believe that God (Allah) would sanction companionship with the White race! To Malcolm, the White race was considered to be devils and ungodly. We African Americans were meant to stay separate from Whites and to unify among ourselves. Nor did God intend for us to take racist abuse lying down. We were called to implement an agenda of Black Liberation, and by any means necessary!

As they were fighting the same fight, the paths of Dr. King and Malcolm X would inevitably cross. Each man appealed to a different consciousness in African Americans. As a result, our community was split. Whom to follow? King, who advocated nonviolent confrontation and peaceful coexistence or Malcolm, the man whose uncompromising rhetoric stirred fear in the hearts of Blacks and Whites? The Christian or the Muslim?

11

The integrationist or the nationalist? After eight years of verbal sparring in the media, these two great African Americans did meet briefly, face-to-face, on March 26, 1964, during the historical March on Washington.

King's movement raised a fundamental issue in the consciousness of Black people: can Black people be both American and African? How should we be identified? Should we identify with our immediate historical origin or our indigenous nation of birth? Malcolm believed that African Americans had to choose, we could not be both. Either you were American and a slave or a true son or daughter of Africa. Malcolm eloquently spoke on this issue numerous times:

> They have contended that 246 years of slavery, followed by legal segregation, social degradation, political disfranchisement, and economic exploitation means that blacks will never be recognized as human beings in White society. America isn't for blacks; blacks can't be for America.[2]

As a Black nationalist, Malcolm believed that African Americans have no place among the White race. White people have enslaved, dehumanized, and killed Black people for generations. Malcolm could envision no other solution than total separation from them. He wanted African Americans to live some place, any place, other than America where we could fully create social and political institutions based on our history and culture. He envisioned an African society in which we would determine our own destiny.[3]

While King's future world had Blacks and Whites living in harmony. Malcolm's philosophy was firmly rooted in a present reality. Every day he witnessed the poverty of Blacks and the brutal way we were treated by Whites. The most significant influence on Malcolm's perception was his religion, Islam. Just as Richard Allen and Absolm Jones defected from the White Methodist Church in 1787 to found the African Methodist Episcopal denomination, the Black Muslim movement was born in Detroit (1930) by Wallace D. Fard and flourished under the leadership of his disciple, a former Baptist minister from Sandersville, Georgia, who answered to the name of Elijah Poole, later renamed Elijah Muhammad.[4] A mystical legend grew up around the founding of the sect. It was believed that Allah ventured to North America in the body of Wallace D. Fard to answer the cries of former slaves and their sons and daughters. Fard rejected Christianity as the White man's religion—a religion that was guilty of dismantling the tribal states of Africa, justifying American slavery, and perpetrating deception and greed throughout the world.

Elijah Muhammad influenced the political consciousness of millions, including his student, Malcolm X, and was the sole, absolute authority in defining the practice and doctrine of the Nation of Islam. According to Muhammad, God (Allah) was Black and the source of all good.[5] He declared that all Whites

were evil by nature. They were snakes, devils, and totally inca-
pable of doing good.[6] White supremacy was the source of African American oppression.

In the Christian worldview, Satan, the devil, is the source
of all evil. According to Muhammad, the Black scientist Yacob
unleashed evil in the world via the White race. White people,
said Muhammad, were created from the remnants of weak members of the African race. White people (Caucasians, Europeans)
were by nature liars, murderers, and human beasts similar to the
Christian devil.[7] Malcolm often called Whites the "enemies of
the truth."[8]

On the other hand, Black people were basically divine
and good by nature. Total separation from the "devil White race"
was only proper and fitting. Malcolm's separatist views originated with his teacher, who actively sought a territory in which
Blacks could live in peace. During the early 1960s, Muhammad
proposed two solutions to the White race problem: (1) Blacks
return to Africa or (2) the U.S. government grant Blacks land
and financing.[9]

Although Malcolm's followers were primarily Muslim,
he did have sympathizers outside Islam. Black Christians were
well aware that 11:00 a.m. on Sunday morning was one of the
most segregated hours of the week. As a result, many in the Black
church began to consider Muhammad's and Malcolm's proposal
for a separate state. As one of the truly independent institutions
in America, the Black church has a distinct cultural and spiritual

identity. It did not want to sacrifice itself to a White Christianity that used scripture to justify slavery and to prove White supremacy over all races.

Malcolm had no patience with Negroes who felt a need to integrate with Whites, and his uncompromising rhetoric struck a cord with many Blacks. He felt that the Negro elite (the college-educated) who desperately sought acceptance by White America was just like the "house niggers" of slavery, always seeking to appease their White masters. All Malcolm could see, however, was the violence of White hate groups, the lynching of Black men in the Southern states, and the discrimination against them in the North. He saw institutional racism as being entrenched within American society and could not reconcile that reality with the weak house Negro. He understood and gave voice to what it was like to be Black in a White racist system.[11]

Malcolm's words created within many African Americans a strong sense of self-worth. He told Blacks that it was more than okay to be dark and the inheritors of a great cultural and intellectual legacy. He reminded Blacks that we were indeed fully human and deserving of self-respect. A community overwhelmed by misery eagerly received his words of encouragement. They provided the spiritual uplifting which was necessary in steering Blacks to healing and a higher quality of life.

Many considered Malcolm's rhetoric to be absolute truth derived from the bottom of the Black experience. His allegiance was Black, his objective was Black. Malcolm would repeatedly affirm his lack of interest in America and was often portrayed as a "messiah of hate" and a "violence-preaching Black Muslim racial agitator."[12] *Time* magazine (February 21, 1965) said that Malcolm seemed unashamed of his hatred of Whites and was a liability to the civil rights movement.

Early Childhood Experiences

Malcolm X was born Malcolm Little on May 19, 1925, in Omaha, Nebraska. Without a doubt, early childhood racial trauma contributed to his belief that the only solution to the White problem was a separate state for the Black man. His childhood memories of the destructive forces of White supremacy were vivid. He blamed his mother's confinement to a mental hospital on White supremacy. He said, "Hence I have no mercy or compassion in me for a society that will crush people and then penalize them for not being able to stand up under the weight."[13]

Another childhood memory contributed to Malcolm's worldview. A brilliant student, Malcolm declared that he wanted to be a lawyer. His White teacher immediately sought to lower his sights. The law just wasn't a fitting profession for a Negro.[14]

Malcolm quickly descended into a world of vice and destruction, and he ended up in prison. It was in prison that he was introduced to and embraced the anti-White, anti-Christian Islamic faith of Elijah Muhammad.[15] After serving his time, Malcolm became Elijah's most effective evangelist as he traveled the U.S., organizing new temples.

Malcolm wrote a weekly column entitled "God's Angry Men," which explored the brainwashed condition of the so-called Negroes who he believed were innocently unaware of the White man's satanic nature.[16] Exposing the truth about the hypocrisy of Northern White liberals ("camouflaged racists") was his primary focus. These traitors, he contended, pretended to be friends with the Black community and eagerly pointed their fingers at the Southern Whites.[17] According to Malcolm, Northern Whites were wolves and Southern Whites were foxes. When choosing between the lesser of the two evils, Malcolm preferred the Southern segregationist who was honest about his hatred of Blacks to the deceptive hypocrisy of the Northern integrationist, who pretended to be the Black man's friend.[18] He said that the Southern rattlesnakes "always let you know where they stand, but the Northern snakes grinned in deceit."[19]

Malcolm saw integration as a White liberal conspiracy, designed to strangle any and all militant efforts to promote freedom, justice, and equality.[20] The viper tongue of this militant Muslim often cut deep to the core of White America as he called Whites "every scurrilous name he could think of including blue-eyed devils, two-legged snakes, international thugs and rapists, White apes and beasts."[21]

Their White flag further enraged Malcolm. This flag offered absolutely no protection for African Americans as could be proved by the historical record.

The White man was guilty of monstrous, hideous crimes against humanity.[22] Indeed, Malcolm perceived the crimes it perpetrated against Blacks as the worst in human history. Using the Bible to enslave and justify violence against Blacks was pure evil. The White race is guilty of murdering 100 million to get at least 15 million Africans to the Americas to use as slaves.[23] Furthermore, this blue-eyed devil began raping the Black woman on the slave ships, thus promoting a campaign of lust, murder, and an orgy of greed uncommon to the civilized world.[24]

Based on his childhood memories, his knowledge of history, and his Black Muslim theology, Malcolm wrote a new agenda for the Black community. He promoted unity, self-knowledge, self-love, self-defense, and most important, separation from Whites.[25] Freedom, love, knowledge, and unity were bound together in his vision.[26] He knew that the path to liberation must include a healing of the neuroses that divided us, a knowledge of our history, and an overhaul of our consciousness. Malcolm sought to liberate us from mental and physical bondage. Self-love and self-defense were inseparable. "Love yourself," he repeatedly told his audiences.[27] Defending oneself during an attack was a God-given right, a moral right, and a human right.[28]

Separation was most important to this fiery Black Muslim. Malcolm believed that Blacks should integrate only with God (Allah) and their own kind. It was an act of self-love to separate from the blue-eyed White man and, devoid of negative White influences, Blacks could begin to love each other. Malcolm said, "If I didn't love you, I wouldn't tell you what I'm telling you. I wouldn't stick my neck out...this is love talk, we love you, but we don't love him [the White man]. We want to unite with you, but we don't want to unite with him."[29]

Justice meant punishing Whites who needed to reap the harvest they had sown against Black people."[30] Integration was a sinking ship and the judgment of the Lord was upon it.[31] Malcolm often reminded Blacks that our humanity did not depend on any form of association with the White race. Unity among our own kind must be established before any form of integration could be attempted. Integration would only result in disunity among African Americans.[32]

Malcolm despised tokenism. He believed that full integration could not occur because Whites were not sincere. *Separation* was quite different from *segregation*. The former is implemented voluntarily. The latter are forced upon people and intentionally labels the victims as inferior and the enforcers as superior.[33]

Malcolm X ministered to Blacks who needed self-respect and an emotional shot in the arm. Most importantly, he taught African Americans that the ideal of a politically and economically autonomous Black community was not beyond the realm of the possible. He taught us to search ourselves for the answers to our most pressing questions and that the White man's interpretation of the Holy Bible was incorrect and questionable.

The White perception of God was no longer applicable to the Black Experience. Malcolm's innovative approach to God and Black culture opened our minds and spirits to a new life-enhancing interpretation of the scriptures. This was needed to find our identity in a foreign land ruled by the White race.

Chapter 3: James Cone

Racism is viewed as a global behavior power system with a constant and specific set of power relationships. Racism evolved with the singular goal of White supremacy or White power domination by the global White minority over the vast non-White global majority. This colored global collective has been forced into the position of relative powerlessness compared to the global White collective establishing the power equation of White over non-White (W/N-W).[1]

Islam's holy book, the Koran, helped Black Muslims sever the umbilical cord connecting them to White oppressors. African American Christians desperately searched their holy book to accomplish the same end. Both Christians and Muslims have searched for a cultural identity within the parameters of their religions.

James H. Cone was the leading light of Black Christianity. He sought a more life enhancing interpretation of the Bible for African Americans. Cone struggled through Garrett-Evangelical Theological Seminary to find new meaning in his religion. He prayed and God answered with his famous Black Liberation Theology.

To understand the influence of Black Liberation Theology on the formation of my African American Liberation Theology, we must first examine the origin of Cone's thought. The three

21

major factors which led to his theory were: (1) the civil rights movement and the emergence of Martin L. King, Jr.; (2) the publication of Joseph Washington's book, *Black Religion,* in 1964; and (3) the rise of the Black Power, Black Nationalism, and Malcolm X.[2]

Black Liberation Theology gave the civil rights movement its foundation, justification, and protest strategies. It was critical to African Americans' struggle for liberation, equality, and justice. Since the White church was silent on the White racial problem, Black theologians, ministers, and lay people were forced to search the scriptures on their own. This was a blessing. Blacks began to "search the scriptures deeply and from the context of their own history to find a sound theological basis for their prior political commitment to liberate the black poor."[3]

The autonomous Black church has led nearly every struggle for liberation waged by Africans in America. God, the Creator, the I AM, who summoned Moses and gave his only Son, Jesus, did not create Africans to be slaves or second-class citizens.[4] That was the revolutionary message of the Black church.

The African American community believed that it was the White church that was hypocritical; White churches intentionally ignored the biblical theme of justice for all. Black Christians began to dismiss the notion that true Christian identity was based on one's ability to engage in theoretical discussion. Instead, Christian belief held that God is essentially the Father of justice and love. He is forever present in times of trouble. He is ever present in the Black struggle for equality and liberation.[5]

Stokley Carmichael popularized the phrase "Black Power" during the spring of 1966, the most turbulent days of the civil rights era.[6] Martin Delany and others in the 1850s initiated the term. It caused quite a stir in both the enemies and supporters of civil rights, especially Dr. King. African American baby boomers were hypnotized by the phrase, and it caused them to swell in pride. Black Power was the complete emancipation from White oppression by whatever means necessary, including civil disobedience, marching, and boycotting.[7]

Black Power was about self-determination. It was about having the ability to implement social, economic, and political strategies. It was about determining one's own destiny. Carmichael stated, "Black Power means T.C.B., Take Care of Business—black folk taking care of black folk business, not on the terms of the oppressor, but on those of the oppressed."[8] To paraphrase theologian Paul Tillich, Black Power gives Black people the courage to affirm their being and to move against any force that attempts to negate it.[9]

For its adherents, Black Power solved the essential problem African Americans suffered, and still continue to suffer. Do we exist or not? Ralph Ellison's *Invisible Man* defined the "to be or not to be" question from a Black experiential point of view. White supremacy sought to destroy our physical bodies and God-given minds, thus rendering us, at the very least invisible and at worst, dead. When it could not completely kill us off, this evil force tried to make us invisible through discrimination and segregation.

Many Negroes had a problem with Black Power because it was loud. It refused to be quiet while oppression existed. It proclaimed our existence with a James Brown beat: "I'm Black and I'm proud!" It was not a subtle declaration but two African American Olympic champions throwing their fists high in defiance as the American flags were raised.

Negroes of the old school tended to be embarrassed by Black Power, but young Black men and women created a new "in your face" style, with Black Power as the foundation. Big afro hair styles and dashikis were the outer signs of an inner revolution that was occurring on high school and college campuses. Many journeyed to Africa, or at the very least studied the land of their ancestors. Historiography was shaken to its core. Europe was no longer the center of the world, Africa was.

Black Power was about shaking off the rags of shame and putting on the dashiki of pride and self-love. For the first time since emancipation, Black Power instilled in African Americans a positive attitude about Blackness. We began to say *yes* to our own Black being and *no* to White supremacy.

This unique form of self-empowerment set the stage for Black Liberation Theology. It was believed that the God of the oppressed began to speak to the African American condition, reaffirming that our blackness was no mistake. Enter James Cone, the young Black theologian who analyzed, critiqued, and developed this personal message from God, which was dispatched from the spiritual throne of grace to the brokenness of our human condition.

The Black Power Movement played a significant role in the formation of Black Liberation Theology. After the unfortunate assassination of Malcolm X on February 21, 1965, the term "Black Power" became an ideal whose time had come.[10] This rise of self-proclaimed power produced a cataclysmic effect within the Black community. The National Committee of Negro Churchmen (NCNC), which would later become known as the National Conference of Black Churchmen (NCBC), publicly refused to denounce the slogan. In fact, NCBC wrote the "Black Power Statement," which appeared in the *New York Times*, July 31, 1966.[11]

The Black Power Statement and the momentum of the civil rights movement conspired to catapult the African American community into a new era of Black consciousness and sparked the beginning of Black Liberation Theology. Black ministers throughout the country began to boldly separate themselves from the old interpretation of scripture that was based on the White perspective. They replaced pictures of White Jesus with Black ones. They began to search our history for a deeper understanding of how God has moved in the African experience and how the Bible could instruct the liberation cause.

It was boldly, publicly suggested for the first time in our torrid history that White Christianity, liberal and conservative, was spiritually and morally bankrupt. The time had come to form our own distinct interpretation of the Gospel, separate from the White man's and linked to our African heritage and struggle for equality and liberation.[12] Black church leaders began to openly denounce White racism as evil. It was in this context that the term "Black theology" emerged.[13]

As Black Christians became more spiritually enlightened, they became the instruments of their own liberation. They called upon White churches throughout the land to eliminate all forms of racism. This was a priority of the Black Power Movement.

The theology of Black Power can be analyzed in many ways—politically, economically, socially. I choose to focus on the spiritual—the eternal love of God for Black people. According to James Cone, God unconditionally loves the Black man (and woman). "God had made him [and her] somebody."[14] This was a new way to think about ourselves. We had become so accustomed to thinking of ourselves as the White man considered us—inferior and subhuman—that Cone's revelation came as a spiritual jolt. This new image allowed us to *become* by giving us the power to recognize ourselves as special creations, loved by God. Our Blackness is special in the sight of God, therefore there's no need to be like others—especially Whites.

To be able to say the Black Power phrases, "I'm Black and I'm proud" and "I'm Black and beautiful," with confidence "means that he [she] accepts the true image of himself [herself] revealed in Jesus Christ."[15]

Throughout the Black consciousness movement, God began to speak to the sons and daughters of enslaved Africans. Under his divine plan, freedom, equality, and liberation manifested from the spiritual realm to the physical. This quest for liberation endured a period of social violence to achieve a personal and social affirmation of being.

God's love enabled us to proclaim our inherent right to exist as free humans and to identify positively with our Blackness. His intervention into America's evil social affairs helped African Americans to defy the odds. Moved by the Holy Spirit, we would achieve individual and collective greatness. This explosion of power under discipleship dramatically affected the spiritual agenda of the African American community.

Cone's spiritual genius resided in the fact that he was able to see how White supremacy had created an unholy alliance between enslavement of Blacks and the Christian Gospel. He believed that our only hope was in Black Liberation Theology. "Thus the task of theology is to show what the changeless gospel means in each new situation."[16] Black Liberation Theology's sole purpose was to use the Gospel to liberate Blacks from White oppression and to assert our existence in a society that tried to render us invisible.[17]

As Cone pondered the Black experience and the Christian gospel, he formulated two important questions. The first question pertains to Black consciousness: How can the Christian gospel renew the minds of African Americans whose existence is threatened daily by the insidious tentacles of White power? Cone said that "the gospel becomes a lifeless message unless its theology can become *ghetto theology* and speak directly to Black people and their struggle for liberation."[18] The second question ponders our Black identity and the idea of blackness as the Ultimate

Reality: "It is impossible for me to surrender this black reality for a higher, more universal reality?"[19]

The Ultimate Reality and our Blackness are intertwined. It is this intimate, divine relationship that was and is the source of our power as a race. African American Liberation Theology affirms that Blacks have never been, nor will they ever be, powerless. Throughout our history it has been the indomitable power of Divine Black Consciousness, bestowed upon us by the Creator, that is responsible for our survival.

The Ultimate Reality is God, *the source of all life*, not our Blackness! It is through our individual and collective consciousness that God empowers us to seek His face. Thus empowered, the Holy Spirit helps us to identify and acknowledge the Creator as the Universal God, interpret and carry out His purpose for our lives, and communicate and develop intimacy with Him. As this holy relationship deepens, we are able to receive His instructions. No movement can succeed without this divine foundation. No movement can succeed without Jesus Christ.

For centuries, the concept of *soteriology* has been debated: the Christian doctrine stands on the premise that due to the fall of man, God the Creator can only be approached through the recognition and acceptance of Jesus Christ, our Lord and Savior.

Every school child learns that to know Jesus Christ as one's personal savior and deliverer leads to the presence of the Ultimate Reality in one's own life. What we have also learned, but have yet put into practice, are that as members of the Body of Christ, we have a responsibility to one another. We must learn to demonstrate peaceful coexistence with humans of all races, animals, and earth's delicate ecosystem if we are to be the messengers of Christ's Gospel throughout the world.

Analysis of the Two Theologies

African American Liberation Theology hypothesizes that certain African Americans are among the chosen people who have received God's eternal purpose through the Gospel of Jesus Christ. Romans 8:28–31 supports this assessment:

We know that all things work for good for those who love God, who are called according to his purpose. For those he foreknew he also predestined to be conformed to the image of his Son, so that he might be the firstborn among many brothers. And those he predestined he also called; and those he called he also justified; and those he justified he also glorified.

African American Liberation Theology and Black Liberation Theology agree on four propositions: God exists, God is all-powerful, God is all-good, evil exists. Both theologies denounce certain shapes of evil against God: the denial of evil (naïve idealism), the denial of God's goodness (Satanism), the bad God (pantheism), the "blob" God (deism), the "snob" God (elitism), many Gods (new scientific paganism), naturalistic God (dualism), the denial of God's reality (atheism), and the fairy tale God (psychology).[20]

On the other hand, our theologies differ in key areas. Cone's sees God as intimately involved in the affairs of humans, particularly the oppressed, but it states little or nothing about God's grace upon the oppressor and His overall intentions of restoring all people to their original state of oneness with the Creator, the Logos. Cone's theology fails to adequately address those African Americans who have made a free-will decision to turn away from God and consciously, willingly enter into a partnership with evil.

While Cone's Black Theology addresses the experience of all oppressed members of the African Diaspora, African American Liberation Theology is exclusive to Blacks in America. I believe that God is pouring out His spirit upon the sons and daughters of former slaves in America, empowering them with the love of Christ that they may become instruments of God's overall plan to reconcile mankind. Cone would disagree, but I believe that God's plan of reconciliation includes White oppressors and defiant, rebellious African Americans—in other words, whosoever will call upon the name of the Lord. The supporting scriptures for this revelation are as follows:

And the Lord appeared to Solomon by night, and said unto him, I have heard thy prayer, and have chosen this place for myself as an house of sacrifice. If I shut up heaven that there is no rain, or if I command the locust to devour the land, or if I send pestilence among my people; If my people, who are called by my name, shall humble themselves, and pray and seek my face, and turn from their wicked ways, then will I hear from heaven, and will forgive their sin, and will heal their land.— 2 Chronicles 7:12–14

And it shall come to pass, when all these things are come upon thee, the blessings and the curse, which I have set before thee, and thou shalt call them to mind among all the nations, whither the Lord thy God hath driven thee, And shalt return unto the Lord thy God, and shalt obey his voice according to all that I command thee this day, thou and thy children, with all thine heart, and with all thy soul; That then the Lord thy God will return thy captivity, and have compassion upon thee, and will return and gather thee from all the nations, whither the Lord thy God hath scattered thee. If any of thine be driven out unto the outmost parts of heaven, from thence will he fetch thee: And the Lord thy God will bring thee into the land which thy fathers possessed, and thou shalt possess it; and he will do thee good, and multiply thee above thy fathers. And the Lord thy God will circumcise thine heart, and the heart of thy seed, to love the Lord thy God with all thine heart, and the heart of thy seed, to love the Lord thy God with all thine heart, and with all thy soul, that thou mayest live. And the Lord thy God will put all these curses upon thine enemies, and on them that hate thee, which persecuted thee. And thou shalt return and obey the voice of the Lord, and do all his commandments which I command thee this day.— Deuteronomy 30:1-8

Regarding the issue of evil, Cone's theology focuses on racism. White racism is the weapon used by those in control to keep minorities permanently oppressed. Racism is "the assumption that psychocultural traits and capacities are determined by biological race and that races differ decisively from one another, which is usually coupled with a belief in the inherent superiority of a particular race and its rights to dominance over others."[21] Thus, the destruction of racism must be the number one priority in the quest for Black liberation.[22] According to Cone, Black suffering at the hands of Whites has little value, and the task of Black Theology is "to destroy White racism."[23] Cone further insists that if Blacks harbor ill feelings against Whites, this cannot be considered racism.[24]

African American Liberation Theology differs from Cone's militant perspective. There are three types of disharmony that separate us from God and the knowledge of ourselves: (1) suffering, the disharmony between our bodies and the world; (2) death, the separation of the soul from the body; and (3) sin, the alienation of the soul from God.[25] African American Liberation Theology identifies White racism as sin, evil, Satan-inspired behavior and thought. White oppression and White power are the tentacles and tools of White racism. White racism operates in corporate, political, religious, and educational institutions. I believe that nothing less than a total dismantling and restructuring of American social systems and laws is needed. This would give guilty Whites an opportunity to repent and reconcile their evil ways with God and all oppressed peoples.

We cannot entertain the idea of White soul destruction. They must be given an opportunity to repent, and we must be able to forgive them. As Luke 15:3–4 says, "And he spoke this parable unto them, saying, What man of you, having an hundred sheep, if he lose one of them, doth not leave the ninety and nine in the wilderness, and go after that which is lost, until he find it."

God's Holy Spirit can revitalize the souls of African Americans and Whites. This new soul will receive forgiveness and eternal life through Jesus Christ. God's spirit will allow us to say *yes* to our Creator, *yes* to our Blackness, *yes* to the beloved community, and *yes* to multiracial companionship. The scale of power will be balanced.

According to Cone, Christ is alive in Black people today. According to African American Liberation Theology, Christ is not only alive in the Black struggle but also in the divine struggle for global human reconciliation. Original Sin, a condition transmitted to the whole human race as a result of the sin of Adam, affects us all.[26] Thus, we must all atone for our racial and human sins against ourselves, each other, and God.

We significantly differ in our perspective of suffering. Cone blames the suffering of Blacks on our White oppressors. He rejects any notion that supports the hypothesis that Black suffering or any form of suffering is the will of God.[27] I can agree— to a point. However, I do believe that suffering has a great deal of meaning and purpose and that despite the pain, we are still graced with God's love and protection.

He that dwelleth in the secret place of the most High shall abide under the shadow of the Almighty. I will say of the Lord, He is my refuge and my fortress: my God; in him will I trust. Surely he shall deliver thee from the snare of the fowler, and from the noisome pestilence. He shall cover thee with his feathers, and under his wings shalt thou trust: his truth shall be thy shield and buckler.— Psalm 91:1–4

Because he hath set his love upon me, therefore will I deliver him: I will set him on high, because he hath known my name. He shall call upon me, and I will answer him: I will be with him in trouble; I will deliver him, and honor him. With long life will I satisfy him, and shew him my salvation.—Psalm 91:14–16

When you are chosen and transformed by the renewing of your spirit, pain and suffering can no longer overtake you, it can no longer seize hold of your nature.[28] I agree with Gabriel Marcel, the existentialist philosopher, who believed that beyond the pains of suffering is new birth.[29]

Cone's theology lacks a framework within which to analyze Black suffering. In theology there are two types of suffering: redemptive and tragic. Redemptive suffering is caused by human injustice. Tragic suffering occurs at death.[30] The Body of Christ, including the Black church, is called to redemptive suffering "in the world, against the world, for the world."[31] And although death faces us all, Christians have the victory over death through the resurrection of Christ.[32]

According to 1 Corinthians 12:26, "If one member suffers, all suffer together. If one member is honored, all rejoice." African Americans share the effects of oppression with the Body of Christ.[33] Thus the Church is motivated to recreate structures of social justice throughout the world.

This fresh perspective embraces the cross and suffering of Christ. According to Holy Scripture, when the pain associated with suffering had reached its extreme on the cross, Jesus cried with a loud voice: *Eli, Eli, lema sabachthani?* Essentially this means, "*My God, my God, why have you forsaken me?*" (Matthew 27:46) And in Matthew 27:50–52,

> But Jesus cried out again in a loud voice, and gave up his spirit. And behold the veil of the sanctuary was torn in two from top to bottom. The earth quaked, rocks were split, tombs were opened, and the bodies of many saints who had fallen asleep were raised.

The suffering (from persecution), death, and resurrection of Jesus imply that suffering and hope cannot be divorced. There is an interdependence between the two.[34] We triumph over sin through the acceptance of the cross; we triumph over death through the acceptance of Christ's resurrection. A theology that denies or underestimates the significance and reality of suffering cannot encompass hope or entertain the possibility of divine intervention which brings about a return to God.

Father Francis Cleary's Old Testament research outlines six types of suffering: retribution, disciplinary, probationary measure, revelational, sacrificial efficacy, and eschatological.[35] From the perspective of African American Liberation Theology, suffering provides opportunities for spiritual growth and redemption. In our sojourn in America, suffering was the catalyst that inspired slave rebellions and the civil rights movement.

The destruction of racism lies at the core of Cone's theology. Death, heaven, and eternal life hold little significance to Cone and are dismissed as fallacies. Furthermore, he sees the war against racism as a fight to the death; Cone is willing to die for its total destruction.[36] According to Cone, the Christian believer must pledge obedience unto death and the cause of Black Liberation.[37]

African American Liberation Theology accepts that death is a part of life. As Jesus Christ, Son of the living God, faced his own death, we certainly cannot eliminate this from our discussion. To negate death is to disregard the importance of the resurrection of Christ. As stated in 1 Corinthians 15:51–55,

> Behold, I show you a mystery: We shall not all sleep, but we shall all be changed, In a moment, in the twinkling of an eye, at the last trump; for the trumpet shall sound, and the dead shall be raised incorruptible, and we shall be changed. For this corruptible must put on incorruption, and this mortal must put on immortality. So, when this corruptible shall have put on incorruption,

and this mortal shall have put on immortality, then shall be brought to pass the saying that is written, Death is swallowed up in victory O Death, where is thy sting? O grave, where is thy victory?

Paul said that the sting of death is sin. Sin, death, and suffering are the evils that Christ came to help us overcome. 1 Corinthians 15:26 identifies death as the last enemy which shall be destroyed. We all know that one day we all must die, but the thought causes fear and panic in our hearts, minds, and souls. The fear of White supremacy was linked to our fear of death. If we did not submit to White injustice, we would die. However, scripture tells us that we should not fear death. The Psalmist says that we can walk in the valley of the shadow of death, fearing no evil. Psalms 89:47–48 says, "Remember how short my time is! Why hast thou made all men in vain? What man is he that liveth, and shall not see death? Shall he deliver his soul from the power of Sheol? Selah."

In our struggle for liberation, we will be confronted with the evils of sin, suffering, and even our own deaths as well as the deaths of our friends and family. However, through Christ, we are overcomers because our suffering and death bring about repentance. Death carries a cosmic significance in that "no one lives, suffers, and dies for himself alone."[38] And in Romans 8:16–17: "The Spirit himself beareth witness with our spirit, that we are the children of God; And if children, then heirs, heirs of God, and joint heirs with Christ—if so be that we suffer with him, that we may be also glorified together."

Dr. King was quite aware of his impending death, but his love for God and neighbor, coupled with his resolve to follow through on his God-given mission, moved him beyond fear and allowed him to see a future free of oppression. Those individuals empowered by God's Holy Spirit can never be preoccupied with the fear of suffering and death. Christ suffered and died. He gave his life so that others could find their way to God. We too must be willing to give our lives in the ongoing struggle for African American liberation. When we promote the love and will of God, we must be willing to display the quiet courage to die, thus proclaiming to the oppressor that the wages of sin is death, but the gift of God is eternal life.

With all due respect to Dr. Cone, I believe that God not only shows Himself on the mountaintop but in the valley of the shadow of death. He is forever with those who find that they are in the basement of their lives.

We are not called to respond to oppression with fear and hatred. Read Matthew 22:36–40:

> Master, which is the greatest commandment in the law? Jesus said unto him, Thou shalt love the Lord, thy God, with all thy heart, and with all thy soul, and with all thy mind. This is the first and greatest commandment. And the second is like it; Thou shalt love thy neighbor as

thyself. On these two commandments hang all the law and the prophets.

In his dying hour, Jesus forgave the thief who asked for forgiveness. "And Jesus said unto him, Verily I say unto thee, Today shalt thou be with me in paradise" (Luke 23:43). In addition to forgiveness, the compassion of Christ empowers us. As He hung from the cross, dying and in pain, Jesus cried to God to forgive his executors. Through the supreme sacrifice of His only begotten Son, we are empowered by God to overcome the sins, sufferings, and death caused by White racism.

Cone's theology is based primarily on the destruction of White racism. Cone believes that liberation for Blacks should come by any means necessary. Cone is theologically negligent regarding the issues of forgiveness, compassion, and love. Witness Luke 6: 27-28: "But I say unto you that hear, Love your enemies, do good to them who hate you. Bless them that curse you, and pray for them who despitefully use you." Unlike Cone, I do not believe that the unearned suffering of African Americans dilutes God's love for those who stumble in the darkness of racism and White supremacy.

Black liberation will manifest as we comprehend, accept, and demonstrate unconditional agape love to ourselves and our oppressors. First and foremost, we must dismantle racial self-hatred and learn to love ourselves. As we draw closer to each other, we draw closer to God. "Man develops forward and upward to God drawing the whole cosmos."[39]

In our quest for African American liberation, we must not embrace the same psychoses and violence used against us by Whites. We must be free of hostility and void of any tendencies toward reverse racism. We must be grounded in the unconditional agape love of Christ. We must be patient and reach out to all those who are burdened by the difficulties of life. We must be willing to carry our own cross and, if need be, the crosses of others. We must be willing to suffer on the cross, and through this suffering seek repentance. We must be willing to forgive those who crucify the innocent. We must even prepare a table in the presence of the enemy. That means having the willingness to face death, the last enemy, and commend our spirits to God. Then God is more than willing to resurrect us from death and grant us eternal life.

Prior to his departure from earth, Jesus prayed to the Father to give us a Comforter (John 14:18). Cone's assessment on suffering and death fail to address this essential promise of Christ. In fact, Cone is not the least bit concerned with the *last things*. His primary focus is the *White thing*. His original version of Black Theology is not spiritual in nature—quite the opposite. Cone admits that "Black Theology is an earthly theology."[40] Cone believes that God is involved in the here and now, not the hereafter. Concentrating liberation efforts on the eternal is foolish and hopeless. Instead, self-determination for Blacks must be the emphasis of a relevant theology.

Cone's theology rejects any notion of a synthesis between this world and God. Eschatology (from a biblical perspective) relates to God's involvement in man's history—what God will do for his people, what God has done, and what God is doing.[41] Cone's theology endorses an eschatology that confronts White racism with Black Power. Eschatology is the realization of hope and justice, the socializing of humanity, the humanizing of man, the peace for all creation in lieu of the salvation of the soul, comfort for the troubled conscience, individual rescue from the evil world.[42] This eschatological hope demands the implementation of creative discipleship armed with the categorical imperative of overthrowing unjustifiable, inhumane acts of oppression.

African American Liberation Theology insists that the future has already begun with Christ. It agrees with Romans 5:12–19: death, suffering, and sin entered the world through Adam, but grace and eternal life entered the world through Christ. Cone and I both agree that God's kingdom breaks through the darkness of this world and represents a ray of hope to those who are oppressed. I agree with Dr. King who once wrote, "Any religion that professes to be concerned with the souls of men and is not concerned with the slums that damn them, the economic conditions that strangle them, and the social conditions that cripple them is a dry-as-dust-religion. Such a religion is the kind the Marxists like to see—an opiate of the people."[43]

African American Liberation Theology promotes the idea that as God enters human history to bring about change, the outcome changes simultaneously. He is indeed the Alpha and the Omega! Here's what scripture says:

Behold, the virgin shall be with child, and shall bring forth a son, and they shall call his name Immanuel, which being interpreted, is God with us."— Matthew 1:23

Who were born not of blood, nor of the will of the flesh, nor of the will of man, but of God. And the Word was made flesh, and dwelt among us (and we beheld his glory, the glory as of the only begotten of the father) full of grace and truth.— John 1:13–14

The birth of Christ interfered with the evil of the day (i.e., sin, suffering, death, racism, oppression) and brought about a ray of hope to the oppressed throughout the world. Christ represents a new beginning of a divinely ordered end for Africans in America and throughout the world. Christ is forever present with us, moving us toward a glorified end to human history which is the final defeat of evil.

The Parousia (i.e., the second coming of Christ) stands as an assurance of divine assistance in the predestined, unavoidable assault by the antichrist upon the Church and God's elect.

And lo, I am with you always even unto the end of the age.—Matthew 28:20

Even him whose coming is after the working of Satan with all power and signs and lying wonders.— Thessalonians 1:9

Little children, it is the last time; and as ye have heard that antichrist shall come, even now are there many

antichrist, by which we know that it is the last time.—
1 John 2:18

For many deceivers are entered into the world,
who confess not that Jesus Christ cometh in the flesh. This
is a deceiver and an antichrist.— 2 John 1:7

In the struggle for African American liberation, we cannot afford to dismiss the biblical writings as ancient nonsense.
African Americans must accept the promise of Christ's return
and His critical re-entry into the final phase of human history. If
we fail to realize racism within the greater context of evil, we
will miss the victory. The antichrist's agenda is the destruction
of the Church as we know it. The African American fight against
racism is but *one* fight against *one* type of sin.

According to Hebrew 11:1, "Faith is the substance of
things hoped for, the evidence of things not seen." African American Liberation Theology agrees with this profound definition of
faith. I also subscribe to the following acronym: F.A.I.T.H—
Forsaking All I Trust Him.

Given the nature of our struggle, we cannot afford to doubt
who we are and *whose* we are. "But ye are a chosen generation,
a royal priesthood, an holy nation, a people of his own, that ye
should show forth the praises of him who hath called you out of
darkness into the marvelous light" (1 Peter 2:9). Thus, we are
bound by a covenant with God to believe in the past, present, and
future doctrine of Jesus Christ. His past (the birth, life, and death)

is the evidence of His entrance into human history; the future (the Parousia) is evidence of His promise of the coming of God's kingdom.

> Of the increase of his government and peace there shall be no end, upon the throne of David, and upon his kingdom, to order it, and to establish it with justice and with righteousness from henceforth even forever. The zeal of the lord of hosts will perform this.—Isaiah 9:7

Cone did address the creation of *new values* and *hope*. He believed that separation from White society would give Blacks the freedom to create new possibilities. He defined freedom as that which occurs inside the individual; it is not in any way dependent upon exterior activities such as marching, picketing, or rioting.[44] Cone believed that Blacks must create their own values that are devoid of racism. Black Theology's new value system must be created with one purpose in mind: "the bringing of the spirit of black self-determination upon the consciousness of Black people."[45] This new cultural ethos among the oppressed will sever the slave's umbilical link with White oppression.

According to Cone, Black Religion and Black Power are inseparable. The destruction of White racism is the goal of both. This goal would be accomplished by destroying the influence of White American Christianity and completely reordering the traditional view of black suffering. Black Religion-Black Power would be based on our need to identify, accept, and embrace the "power first to be Black," which would usher in a new era of hope for the voiceless.[46]

African American Liberation Theology disagrees. Suffering and repentance must be included into the equation if we are to achieve liberation. It is essential that our spirits be broken and renewed by God. This is a spiritual quest: "We wrestle not against flesh and blood, but against principalities, against powers, against the rulers of the darkness of this world, against spiritual wickedness in high places" (Ephesians 6:12).

According to Peter Kreeft, author of *Making Sense Out of Suffering*, "The meaning and purpose of suffering in history is that it leads to repentance."[47] Kreeft states that nations only turn to God after disaster or some form of suffering. Suffering also brings about a spiritual and social cleansing. This cleansing becomes fertile soil for the creation of new values; these new values represent hope: "For we are saved by hope. But hope that is seen is not hope; for what a man seeth, why doth he yet hope for? But if we hope for that which we see not, then do we with patience wait for it" (Romans 8:24–25).

African American Liberation Theology views our plight and ultimate resurrection within the six historical cycles (suffering, repentance, blessedness, luxury, pride, and disaster[48]) and the three Christian cycles (persecution, crucifixion, and resurrection). Both cycles are grounded in hope.

Cone dismisses the value of suffering, but I agree with Paul, who believed that the Church is the birthplace of hope. This hope is only made possible because the oppressed (African Americans) can overcome suffering through the death and resurrection of Christ, also known as "the Suffering Servant." Christ's suffering had a purpose—the creation of the Church and the holy mechanism for the cleansing of sins. The Black church also provides fertile soil for new values and hope.

The new values which Cone speaks of can only come by way of Christ. He alone is our hope. The new values bestowed upon African Americans by God incorporate not only a love for God and self but also a need for repentance. Self-righteousness and the myopic view of African American suffering must be replaced with a forgiving spirit toward the White oppressor.

The civil rights movement represented the apex of God's empowerment of African Americans and His chastisement of White America. Embedded in the movement was a command to synthesize the theologies of King, Malcolm, and Cone. With these spiritual giants fighting for the holy cause of Black liberation, there could be no division, chaos, or confusion in the realm of spirit. God is not limited by the petty divisions of men and is more than able to synthesize their theologies, extracting the best of each to take us all to a higher level. This spiritual synthesis combined integration, separation, and nationalism with the beloved community. This synthesis—African American Liberation Theology—has emerged as the new option, offered by God, the

Creator, to African Americans in their pursuit of liberation and racial equality. Just as God delivered the biblical characters of old from oppression, He delivers us today.

No longer can we be defined by White society. Thanks to the contributions of King, Malcolm, and Cone, African Americans began to accept the beauty of their Blackness as a gift from a loving Creator.[49] It is within the context of this special relationship between African Americans and God that we can now explore the synthesis and next evolutionary step in Black religious thought—African American Liberation Theology.

PART II
The Next Step –
African American Liberation Theology

Chapter 1: African American Liberation Theology

One common denominator connecting King, Malcolm, and Cone is that their ministries were *social*. With all due respect to these men and their groundbreaking efforts to address the social, economic, and spiritual needs of Black people, African American Liberation Theology (the Theology) insists that first and foremost, integration should focus on deepening the spiritual relationship with God. Integration is more of a spiritual imperative than a social one. Social integration will be successful only if we establish a rapport with God first. As our personal relationship with God becomes strong, so will our social relationships. It is during prayer and meditation that we receive guidance from God on how to interact with our brothers and sisters.

Our identity resides in our Christianity first, our African roots second. We will continue to flounder as a race if we do not get our priorities in order. God first, social relationships second. It is our relationship with God that births within us our self-esteem. All ego gratification built on the glory received from others is destined to fail. Only God can make us feel good about our Black selves and our Black culture. It is all or nothing: integrate with God first and we ensure our beingness in eternity. Integrate with man first, and we are rendered invisible, nonexistent.

The Theology encompasses the three steps of salvation, deliverance, and liberation demonstrated by Jesus: persecution, crucifixion, and resurrection. Read about Jesus' life in the New Testament, and you will find just how difficult it is to walk this path. We cannot survive this path without Black Power, i.e., *God power*.

The Five Tenets of African American Liberation Theology

1. Black Power comes from God. Divine Black Power, or "soul force," as Dr. King called it, enabled African Americans to channel the frustration of daily degradation and humiliation into a constructive force for change. Power is strength in action. Power is neither good nor evil. Thus, it is essential that in our quest for power we seek guidance from God so that our power is never misdirected and that it is always a force for good.

James Cone's position on power conflicts with the New Testament paradigm. Cone says that Black Power is not Black racism or Black hatred. In the quest for freedom, Blacks themselves will be their own catalyst for liberation. "Black self-determination and Black self-identity" is Black Power; this power allows Blacks "full participation in the critical social, political, and economic decision making process which affect our lives."[1]

Cone says that to be empowered means full participation in the decision making process. He fails to realize that power that operates outside the safeguard of God's love is sinful. Whites fully participate in the decision making process, yet they misuse their power. Power must be tempered by God's Holy Spirit. Still, Cone understands that "the Holy Spirit is the power of God at work in the world effecting in the life of His people His intended purposes."[2] "Furthermore, "the spirit of God is power, power with a moral emphasis."[3]

2. As we struggle for liberation, we must seek God's will on the issues of integration and separation. To disobey divine instructions would be foolish. For example, the children of Israel, having escaped Egyptian rule, waited to receive divine instructions at the foot of Mt. Sinai.

In the third month, when the children of Israel were gone forth out of the land of Egypt, the same day came they into the wilderness of Sinai. For they were departed from Rephidim, and were come to the desert of Sinai, and had pitched in the wilderness, and there Israel camped before the mount. And Moses went up to God, and the Lord called unto him out of the mountain, saying, Thus shalt thou say to the house of Jacob, and tell the children of Israel; Ye have seen what I did unto the Egyptians, and how I bare you on eagle's wings, and brought you unto myself. Now therefore, if ye will obey my voice indeed, and keep my covenant, then ye shall be a peculiar treasure unto me above all people: for all the earth is mine: And ye shall be unto me a kingdom of priests, and a holy nation. These are the words which thou shalt speak unto the children of Israel.— Exodus 19: 1–6

African Americans are very much like the children of Israel. We too were an enslaved people under the rule of a cruel master. Our exodus was the Emancipation Proclamation. The lesson from scripture is clear. It is impossible to achieve true liberation from oppression without first seeking the will of almighty God.

3. The children of Israel were a peculiar people, and so must African Americans maintain their distinctness. In the context of African American Liberation Theology, peculiar means different and unique. Scripture reveals that God's laws, while imposing order, also helped the Israelites maintain their cultural integrity. They were not to take on the ways and worship styles of the Romans or any other oppressor. We African Americans must also seek to retain our cultural uniqueness. Our strength comes not from taking on the ways of Whites but staying true to the worship styles of our forefathers and foremothers.

4. We receive Divine Black Power through God's special anointing. To erase the psychological scars that were engraved on our psyches during slavery and to bring about a collective psychological resurrection, we must be open to the inflow of the Holy Spirit in our individual lives and in our communities. After all that we've been through, our minds and spirits are in desperate need of spiritual renewal and resurrection.

5. Only God can move, motivate, and liberate the soul. When the soul is moved by God, it is instructed to take authority over the dark forces of evil which dare oppose God, the giver of life. The activities of King, Malcolm, and Cone demonstrate that one soul can make a difference. A soul's actions can cause ripple effects throughout the cosmos. The suffering African Americans have endured is undeserved and unearned. Suffering leads to grace, i.e., the liberation of the soul.

This theology teaches that intimate communion with God leads to several powers necessary for life in America—the power to act wisely, the power to discern truth from lies, the power to move in self-acceptance and self-love. In an encounter with God, feelings of inferiority can be healed. No longer do we have to languish in substandard conditions of mind, body, and environment. We are empowered to think for ourselves and determine our own destiny.

African Americans must learn how to be obedient to the will of God. We can trace many of the problems in our communities—drugs, violence, etc.—to slavery and since then, systematic attacks on our people. On the other hand, we often conspire with our enemies toward the end of our own destruction. *We* put the needle in our veins and sell drugs to our children. *We* spend our money on unnecessary material goods. *We* drink the alcohol. *We* pull the trigger against our brothers and sisters. *We* spend our hard earned dollars on every foolish product and unnecessary service. As we seek God's will on every issue, we must put aside our childish rebelliousness. When God speaks, we must become obedient and do what God says.

Only then will we African Americans give birth to a positive reality—the promise of our race and the hope of our ancestors. Our obedience to God must be absolute and continuous. We must acknowledge, praise, and worship God. Even when life looks most bleak, we must, "Through Jesus, therefore…continually offer to God a sacrifice of praise" (Hebrews 13:15). God is our liberator and our redeemer. He is more than worthy to be praised. If we can put aside our egos and our anguish, we will be receptive to receiving God's agenda for our lives.

Separatism and Integration

The beauty of this Theology is that separatism and integration can both be used as effective strategies in our quest for liberation. Separatism enables us to identify and organize around common issues. We can integrate with mainstream American society in order to work, worship, and live. King, Malcolm, and Cone were right. King's entire effort was designed to pave a path for us into all American institutions. Malcolm and Cone said that we must be strong within ourselves as a people.

Many people today believe that integration has hurt us. We have $530 billion dollars in income, and most of it leaves our community as soon as it is earned. When segregation laws kept us out of the mainstream, we were forced to do business with one another. Our dollars circulated within our community. On the other hand, if Malcolm's and Cone's separatism was combined with King's integration, we would be unstoppable. King's integration might allow us to work within corporate America, but Malcolm's and Cone's separatism would encourage us to spend from Black stores, provide scholarships for Black students, tithe to Black churches, build in Black neighborhoods.

It is not racist to separate from other groups to strengthen our relationships and to determine our own destiny. It is insanity *not* to do so. All racial groups convene from time to time for this purpose. When other races get together, we all admire their unity. When African Americans get together, we are called racist. There is a double standard in America, but we cannot afford to let it stop us from doing what we must do—unify around issues of concern.

If any fault can be found with Dr. King's desire for full integration, it is that he did not take Malcolm and Cone seriously enough. We needed to become one with each other first before integrating with others. We needed to learn how to love ourselves and one another first before desiring to imitate White people. We needed to learn the value of our Black perception before seeing the world through White eyes.

Cultural integrity is maintained with a separatist strategy, while tolerance for others is created through integration. To maintain sanity and peace, the two must go hand in hand. Separatism without integration creates bigotry. Integration without separatism creates self-hatred and idol worship. In the African American experience, the idol has been White people.

Cultural integrity is critical in creating legacy and continuity of customs, worship styles, and traditions. If we are unsure of our culture because we have sought to integrate without the benefit of separatism, our children will be confused. This is what we are seeing today. Our children do not know, nor do they appreciate, our history—not just in America, but Africa. They don't know that we were the First People of the earth, the first movers and shakers, the first builders, artists, business people, doctors, educators, scientists, and inventors. Cultural traditions, reinforced through rites of separatism, remind us of the legacy and teach young people.

Integration promotes an ecumenical relationship among all Christian denominations. This is necessary for the spiritual evolution of the Body of Christ. I believe that Christian integration will place African Americans in a strategic position on the global stage to disseminate the will of God in the new millennium. As the first people of the earth, it is our responsibility to bring the earth back to wholeness and health. We must be on the forefront of healing the environment, stopping wars among tribes and nations, and developing new technologies that will create wealth and a high quality of life.

Throughout our history, African Americans have suffered Christ's path of persecution and crucifixion. However, God, who hears the cries of the oppressed, can and will resurrect us, i.e., heal our minds, bodies, and souls.

Cone said, "As long as man is a slave to another power, he is not free to serve God with mature responsibility. He is not free to become what he is—human."[4] To seek God is to seek the Ultimate Reality. It is within this Reality that humans can receive divine guidance and energy for change. Divinely orchestrated Black rebellion is nothing less than God's participation in the affairs of humans. The purpose of Black rebellion is liberation.[5]

This manifestation of God was present during the slave rebellions and the civil rights era. This power has manifested in many men and women, including, Harriet Tubman, Fannie Lou Hamer, Rosa Parks, Malcolm X, Dr. King, James Cone, and Stokely Carmichael.

God Himself empowered the minds, hearts, souls, and conscious of Blacks and Whites. Rebellion was stimulated by the idea "that though God's Ultimate Kingdom be in the future, yet even now it breaks through like a ray of light upon the darkness of the oppressed..."[6]

African American Liberation Theology takes us back to the essence of our being and the foundation of our creation:

> And the Lord God formed man of the dust of the ground, and breathed into his nostrils the breath of life; and man became a living soul.— Genesis 2:7

> And the Lord God caused a deep sleep to fall upon Adam, and he slept: and he took one of his ribs, and closed up the flesh instead thereof; And the rib, which the Lord God had taken from man, made he a woman. And brought her unto the man. And Adam said, This is now bone of my bones, and flesh of my flesh: she shall be called Woman, because she was taken out of Man.— Genesis 2: 21–23

King, Malcolm, and Cone firmly believed in and never doubted their African origins. They did not doubt their calling to preserve the Black race. God summoned their opposing ideologies and caused them to intersect within African American Liberation Theology.

Thanks to the omniscience and omnipresence of God, the ruling class intention of enforcing absolute authority through oppression was derailed.

> I am the God of thy father, the God of Abraham, the God of Isaac, and the God of Jacob. And Moses hid his face; for he was afraid to look upon God. And the Lord said, I have surely seen the affliction of my people which are in Egypt, and have heard their cry by reason of their taskmaster; for I know their sorrow; And I am come down to deliver them out of the hand of the Egyptians, and to bring them up out of that land unto a good land and a large, unto the place of the Canaanites, and the

Hittites, and the Amorites, and the Perizzites, and the Hivites and the Jebusites. Now therefore, behold, the cry of the children of Israel is come unto me: and I have also seen the oppression wherewith the Egyptians oppressed them. Come now therefore, and I will send thee unto Pharaoh, that thou mayest bring forth my people the children of Israel out of Egypt.— Exodus 3:6–10

God is bestowing upon the ex-slaves of the African Diaspora their fair share of power, citizenship, and civil rights in America. Thus, the beloved community is possible. Indeed, it is in the process of becoming a force for good throughout the world.

African Americans are charged by God to assist in the implementation of a more just society. White supremacy must be confronted and dismantled by African Americans who have gained power, authority, and respectability.

In conclusion, contemporary theologians from Jurgen Moltman to Karl Barth agree that the present day theological task should be one which "speaks from within the covenant community with the sole purpose of making the gospel meaningful to the times in which men live. While the gospel itself does not change, every generation is confronted with new problems, and the gospel must be brought to bear on them."[7] Furthermore, the major task of theology is to specifically show what the changeless gospel of Jesus Christ means in each new situation. With his Black

Liberation Theology, James Cone showed us how to receive that revelation. African American Liberation Theology demonstrates how to apply the revelation to positive change.

Chapter 2:   Separatism, Integration, and Nationalism

> Consequently, the missionary proclamation of the cross of the Resurrected One is not an opium of the people which intoxicates and incapacitates, but the ferment of new freedom. It leads to the awakening of that revolt which, in the 'power of the resurrection'...follows the categorical imperative to overthrow all conditions in which man is a being who labors and is heavy laden.[1]

So far we have examined God's movement in the African American experience. With the debut of Black Power, God would show the world His power through the most oppressed race on earth, African Americans. With the intent of defeating the forces of racism and oppression, God orchestrated the following events: the scattering of African people around the globe, the introduction of Christianity to African Americans, the Emancipation Proclamation and the Civil War, post-Reconstruction establishment of Jim Crow laws, World Wars I and II, the Great Migration of Blacks to the North, the Civil Rights Acts of 1875 and 1883, the Plessy v. Ferguson decision, Brown v. Board of Education of Topeka, and the emergence of Islam. The philosophies of Dr. King, Malcolm X, and Dr. Cone were directly shaped by these events.

The polarization of King's, Malcolm's, and Cone's philosophies centered on theological applications of the liberating message of the gospel of Jesus Christ. This phenomenon was particularly compounded by James Cone's integration of the gospel and Black Power and Malcolm's refusal to accept Christianity at all.

In these post-civil rights days, we have returned to a state of stagnation. We are more concerned with watching movies and buying CDs than organizing. Now that we are, more or less, fully integrated into society, we now, more than ever, need the wisdom of King, Malcolm, and Cone to bring us together, not tear us apart.

Old Testament

African American Liberation Theology, the synthesis of these three men's philosophies, has a strong biblical foundation, for it is in the Old and New Testaments where we can learn from the ancients and receive God's word for our lives.

So far I've discussed the persecution, crucifixion, and resurrection of Jesus Christ, however, the message of liberation can also be found in the Old Testament stories. The liberating power of God's spoken word crosses all timelines and cultures. God's word does not just belong to the Christians, the Jews, or the Muslims. Throughout time, it is just that sort of claim that has created wars and strife. God's word is for all people.

The similarities between African Americans and the children of Israel are startling, and thus, we can learn much from their experiences. For example, in Exodus 14:13–14,

> And Moses said unto the people: fear ye not, stand
> still, and see the salvation of the Lord, which He will work

for you today, for whereas ye have seen the Egyptians today, ye shall see them again no more forever. The Lord will fight for you and ye shall hold your peace.

"Stand still and see the salvation of the Lord" has become a classic phrase for African Americans in their quest for liberation.

In Exodus 19:1–8 is another Old Testament message of liberation:

> In the third month after the children of Israel were gone forth out of the land of Egypt, the same day came they into the wilderness of Sinai. And when they were departed from Rephidim, and were come to the wilderness of Sinai; they encamped in the wilderness; and there Israel encamped before the mount. And Moses went up unto God, and the Lord called unto him out of the mountain, saying: thus shalt thou say to the house of Jacob, and tell the children of Israel: Ye have seen what I did unto the Egyptians, and how I bore you on eagles' wings, and brought you unto myself. Now therefore, if ye will hearken unto My voice indeed, and keep My covenant, then ye shall be Mine own treasure from among the people; for all the earth is Mine; and ye shall be unto Me a kingdom of priests, and a holy nation. These are the words which thou shalt speak unto the children of Israel. And Moses

came and called for the elders of the people, and set before them all these words which the Lord commanded him. And all the people answered together, And said: All that the Lord hath spoken we will do. And Moses reported the words of the people unto the Lord.

African American Liberation Theology affirms that after persecution and crucifixion there is resurrection (i.e., liberation). Supporting scripture for God's deliverance of His people can be found in Isaiah 43:14–21:

Thus said the Lord, your redeemer, the Holy One of Israel: for your sake I have sent to Babylon, and I will bring down all of them as fugitives, Even the Chaldeans, in the ships of their shouting. I am the Lord, your Holy One, The Creator of Israel, your King. Thus saith the Lord, who maketh a way in the sea, And a path in the mighty waters; who bringeth forth the chariot and horse, the army and the power; they lie down together, they shall not rise, They are extinct, they are quenched as a wick: Remember ye not the former things, Neither consider the things of old. Behold, I will do a new thing; Now shall it spring forth, shall ye not know it? I will even make a way in the wilderness, And rivers in the desert. The beast of the field shall honor Me, the jackals and the ostriches; Because I give waters in the wilderness, and rivers in the desert, to give drink to My people, Mine elect; the people which I formed for Myself, that they might tell of My praise.

In closing out this perspective on Old Testament messages of liberation I am reminded of God's promise to Jerusalem after the Jews were scattered. This divine message can be found in Isaiah 62:4–9:

> Thou shalt no more be termed Forsaken, neither shall this land any more be termed Desolate: but thou shalt be called, Hephzi-bah, and thy land Beu-lah: for the Lord delighteth in thee, and thy land shall be married. For as a young man marrieth a virgin, so shall thy sons marry thee: and as the bridegroom rejoiceth over the bride, so shall thy God rejoice over thee. I have set watchmen upon thy walls, O Jerusalem, which shall never hold their peace day nor night: ye that are make mention of the Lord, keep not silence, And give Him no rest, till he establish, and till He make Jerusalem a praise in the earth. The Lord hath sworn by his right hand, and by the arm of his strength, Surely I will no more give thy corn to be meat for thine enemies; and the sons of the strangers shall not drink thy wine, for the which thou hast laboured: But they that have gathered it shall eat it, and praise the Lord; and they that brought it together shall drink it, in the courts of my holiness.

New Testament

According to 1 Corinthians 12:4–11:

> Now there are diversities of gifts, but the same
> Spirit. And there are differences of administrations, but
> the same Lord. And there are diversities of operations,
> but it is the same God which worketh in all. But the mani-
> festation of the Spirit is given to every man to profit withal.
>
> For to one is given by the Spirit the word of wis-
> dom; To another the word of knowledge by the same
> Spirit; To another faith by the same Spirit; To another
> the gift of healing by the same Spirit; To another the
> working of miracles; To another prophecy; To another
> discerning of spirits; To another divers kinds of tongues;
> To another interpretation of tongues. But all these worketh
> that one and the sameself Spirit, dividing to every man
> severally as he will.

Once these gifts become manifest in our lives, we become empowered. A spiritual and physical metamorphosis takes
place within the mind, body, and soul of African Americans.

The metamorphosis is processed through the persecution,
crucifixion, and resurrection stages of the Christian walk. We
die and then we are reborn. This process cannot take place without the active presence of the Holy Spirit. Cone saw the Holy

Spirit as pure New Testament, but I believe that the Holy Spirit was revealed in both Old and New Testaments.

According to Genesis 1:1–3,

> In the beginning God created the heaven and earth. And the earth was without form, and void; and darkness was upon the face of the deep. And the Spirit of God moved upon the face of the waters. And God said, let there be light: and there was light.

According to John 1:12–14,

> But as many as received him, to them gave he power to become the sons of God, even to them that believe on his name: Which was born, not of blood, nor of the will of the flesh, nor of the will of man, but of God. And the Word was made flesh, and dwelt among us, (and we beheld his glory, the glory as of the only begotten of the Father,) full of grace and truth.

Divine Black Power is not just a reaction to White racism but a necessary social corrective engineered by God. Racism is

> A power relationship or struggle between groups of people who are competing for resources and political power. It is one group's use of wealth and power and

resources to deprive, hurt, injure, and exploit another group to benefit itself. Racism in practice never existed on earth until the 16th century when White nations began to commercially enslave black people.[2]

Racism is a sin and the source of much evil in the world. Even the World Council of Churches agrees with this assessment.[3] However, where there is sin, there is the opportunity for repentance and atonement. This is where the New Testament comes in.

Cone described Jesus Christ as follows: "He is God Himself coming into the very depths of human existence for the sole purpose of striking off the chains of slavery, thereby freeing man from ungodly principalities and powers that hinder his relationship with God."[4] The critical focus of Jesus' work is liberation. This gospel frees those who are oppressed and enslaved.

Cone's revelation was a radical departure from the Christianity that was taught by Whites. He believed that if Jesus is Lord of the privileged, the rich, White people, "Then the gospel is a lie."[5] But the gospel is truth. Cone saw modern parallels with the beneficiaries of Jesus' ministry. Jesus ministered to the sick and needy; Black people definitely qualify. He fought on behalf of the oppressed; Black people are the modern day children of Israel, dealing with the rule of an evil empire. According to Cone, Christianity is Black Power.

If Cone erred, it was in his failure to identify the source of Black Power as God. Malcolm believed that African Americans should achieve liberation "by any means necessary." Black Power, devoid of God's influence, becomes warped. Senseless violence occurs as a result. Violence must never be initiated simply as a reaction to White racism. African Americans must humble themselves under the nurturing arms of God's Holy Spirit. Black Power without God's influence has resulted in self-imposed exile (segregation) among some African Americans and mindless integration among others.

Free Will

Cone's theology does not address the idea of free will. African American Liberation Theology does. We are free to liberate ourselves from the bonds of oppression by any means necessary—however, is it wise to do so? Yes, God allows us to choose our methods and strategies, but how will we choose? Through undisciplined anger and fear, or by seeking God's will? The paradox—free will humans giving up their free will for God's will—challenges our emotions and our ego needs. Yet, if we can discipline our spirits to listen, receive, and obey God's will, we will see a change in our community.

Cone takes a very narrow interpretation of integration. He believes that integration with Whites means to admit their moral superiority; thus, African Americans should not integrate with them.

African American Liberation Theology, on the other hand, sees no conflict in a lifestyle that encompasses both integration and separatism. African Americans are not confined to one response. God can and will honor all sincere efforts of African Americans to strengthen our cultural foundation through separatism while integrating into the family of humanity. God empowers us with a socio-theological option.

In the arena of White racism, Cone asks, "Is there an appropriate response?" He believed that any response Blacks might give is nothing more than a survival reaction to White oppression. Cone supports the assessment of Lerone Bennett who states, "There is no Negro problem in America; there has never been a Negro problem in America—the problem of race in America is a White problem."[6] Black Power could mean outright rebellion if Whites refuse to get off our backs.[7]

Regardless of the atrocities perpetrated by Whites upon the oppressed, God plans to reconcile the whole of humanity unto Himself. He can and will use the oppressed as ambassadors of love to teach Whites an unforgettable lesson in humility, forgiveness, and atonement. The evil in each and every race will be sifted out, as His people will choose either integration or separation. This is God's will.

Cone's approach to Black liberation is based on the fallacy that all African Americans presently enjoy a state of spiritual solidarity. There is a spiritual schism among Blacks that Cone did not address. We are present in nearly every religious body, from

Christianity to Islam to Buddhism. African American Liberation Theology offers an in-depth analysis of these critical issues— issues which must be addressed if African Americans choose to move toward liberation.

The Emergence

So far, we've discussed the ways in which African American Liberation Theology synthesizes the philosophies of King, Malcolm, and Cone in order to free us from oppression. There is an even more profound agenda for this Theology: God's plan for human reconciliation.

Reconciliation does not mean sameness and acculturation. For too long, White culture has been the standard, but as stated previously, African Americans must retain their cultural identity. Through the blessing of African American Liberation Theology, God proposes that African Americans begin to embrace the ethos of equal and separate rather than separate but equal. Equal and separate offers nationalists the option to stand apart from Whites and to develop the African American community.

For more than four hundred years, separate but equal really meant separate and inferior. During the civil rights era, however, the notion of equality (i.e., equal and separate) found fertile soil as God shaped, molded, and refined our struggling Black culture.

Civil rights for African Americans became an idea whose time had come. During the long night of slavery a new consciousness had been incubating—a positive, proud Black consciousness fueled

71

by Divine Black Power. This spiritual consciousness, bestowed upon us by God, became a powerful defense against assimilation and acculturation. It enabled us to integrate into or separate away from the White race without fear of entering a state of *non-being*.

In fact, the Black church rose to prominence because of the racism of the White church. (Ku Klux Klan members call themselves "Christians.") The racist White church, along with America's political, educational, and economic institutions, did not want to let go of their separate but equal position. Removed from the mainstream of American society, African Americans were forced to cultivate their history and culture and form a spirit of solidarity. According to Cicero, the first century Roman writer, orator, and statesman:

> There is very little that is more important for any people to know than their history, culture, traditions and language; for without such knowledge, one stands naked and defenseless before the world."[8]

Separate and equal emerged out of the philosophy of Dr. King during the spring of 1968. He began to move toward his own synthesis with Malcolm and Cone. King began to see how his "romantic integration…would allow White liberals to pre-serve the reins of political and economic power."[9] Dr. King said,

There are times when we must see segregation as a temporary way-station to a truly integrated society. There are many Negroes who feel this; they do not see segregation as the ultimate goal. They do not see separation as the ultimate goal. They see it as a temporary way-station to put them into a bargaining position to get to that ultimate goal, which is a truly integrated society where there is shared power.[10]

African Americans are no longer passive observers and participants in society. We now possess the intellectual and spiritual competence to participate in and contribute to any activity that affects us. Our consciously intentioned equal and separate strategy gave birth to the autonomous Black church, a force to be reckoned with. The Black church has produced some of the greatest spiritual giants, male and female, the world has ever known.

No longer is the African American community knocking on the doors of the White church, hoping and praying for acceptance. We now have the power, Divine Black Power, to stand on our own feet, interpret the scriptures, engage in theological discourse, and most important, investigate the accuracy of biblical teachings for ourselves.

Total Black liberation begins with the knowledge that African Americans are now and always have been equal to Whites. Sharing power with Whites is critical if we are to raise the quality of life for ourselves, our families, and community.

Total Black liberation means freedom from the bondage of White oppression. This freedom allows us to reconcile with Whites as equals. Reconciliation with Whites does not deny the existence and the rights of White humanity but empowers African Americans to meet Whites (who have repented) on equal ground.[11] Total Black liberation is not dependent on White acceptance of African Americans. On the contrary, it is solely based on divine justice. Through divine justice, African American liberation is more than a composite of our individual and collective human efforts and goals. It is a divine movement on behalf of oppressed African Americans.[12]

According to Gayraud S. Wilmore, African Americans need to regain a sense of cultural vocation. Wilmore believes that this empowerment will come through both a spiritual formation and social transformation.[13] This cultural vocation (which is equivalent to collective and individual spiritual agendas) is based on a divine call, "a life long pursuit in response to God's word—to be free."[14]

Malcolm X also evolved in his philosophy. After his departure from the Nation of Islam, he expressed views similar to King regarding shared power, integration, and separation. Malcolm said, "Integration is only a method that is used by some groups to obtain freedom, justice, equality and respect as human beings. Separation is only a method that is used by other groups to obtain freedom, justice, equality or human dignity."[15]

Thus, the politics of integration began to complement the culture of separation.[15] Moreover, both philosophies served as a means to an end for achieving a Black liberation that includes redefined, restructured social relations as they pertain to the sharing of power.

African American Liberation Theology asks, and answers, two important questions: "What does it mean to be separate if one does not have control over the means of producing and distributing necessities for the survival of the community? Second, What does it mean to integrate with Whites if one does not share decision making power and simultaneously realize communal Black liberation?"[17]

Cultural, political, and economic liberation through the new Theology are an ideal whose time has come. African Americans can be empowered to relate to Whites on equal ground. "One-on-one interactions between individuals from different races complement the safeguarding of Black folks' group interest for liberation."[18]

The distinguished theologian, Dwight N. Hopkins, eloquently stated in *Shoes That Fit Our Feet,*

> No longer will integration mean Blacks sitting with White folks while the latter keep power. Instead, true Black-White integration will work only when the existing White power structure is abolished and, simultaneously,

the African American community secures the right to self-determination (for example the right to temporary separation).[19]

Chapter 3: The Roots of African American Consciousness

> To say No means that the oppressor has overstepped His bounds, and that 'there is a limit beyond which [he] shall not go.' It means that oppression can be endured no longer in the style that the oppressor takes for granted. To say No is to reject categorically 'the humiliating orders of the master' and by so doing to affirm that something which is placed above everything else, including life itself. To say No means that death is preferable to life, if the latter is devoid of freedom. 'Better to die on one's feet than to live on one's knees.' This is what Black Power means.[1]

This chapter will offer a brief exegesis on seven critical aspects of the importance of Black Power-Black Consciousness in the quest for African American liberation.

From the White perspective, Black Power and Black Consciousness have been associated with random violence, insurrections, and impromptu race riots. This assessment focuses on the social reaction and not the cause. Be that as it may, Black Power-Black Consciousness can demonstrate the African American's maturity, a discipline under power. This disciplined Black Power-Black Consciousness has been incubating under the anointing of the Holy Spirit.

We've discussed Black Power-Black Consciousness quite a bit in this book, but let's define it even further. Black Power-Black Consciousness is:

1. An affirmation of our inalienable African humanity.
2. A social corrective designed to combat the forces of racism.
3. A necessary social corrective designed to combat the forces of racism.
4. A defense against the state of non-being.
5. A weapon in the quest for African American liberation.
6. A potent spiritual weapon in our quest for African American liberation.
7. A catalyst that stimulates positive self-identity.
8. A defense against genocide.
9. A corrective for self-hatred.

The most critical component of African American Liberation Theology is Black Power-Black Consciousness. Black Power-Black Consciousness evolved from the Black church, various militant ideologies (including the Black Panther movement), and cultural nationalism (e.g., Maulana Karenga and Amiri Baraka).[2]

Up until now I have discussed Black Power alone, but really, there can be no Black Power without Black Consciousness just as there can be no Black Power without God's influence. As we seek God's will in achieving liberation, our consciousness (i.e., awareness and perception) receives wisdom and the power of discernment.

Every great movement throughout history has begun in the consciousness of the people. God operates in that consciousness.

The spiritual gift of Black Power-Black Consciousness reinforces equal and separate, an important aspect of African American Liberation Theology.

Without a true sense of self there can be no serious move toward Black liberation. This sense of self comes from contact with God, the Creator. It is through this contact that we receive a sense of cosmic partnership. As the Lord declares in Luke 4:18–19, bruised humanity receives a healing balm.

> The spirit of the Lord is upon me, because he has anointed me to preach the gospel to the poor. He has sent me to heal the brokenhearted to preach deliverance to the captives and recovering of sight to the blind, to set at liberty them that are bruised, to preach the acceptable year of the Lord.

The Old Testament theme of liberation is also applicable as God declared unto Moses in Exodus 3:7:

> And the Lord said, I have surely seen the affliction of my people which are in Egypt, and have heard their cry by reason of their taskmasters; for I know their sorrows.

God empowers African Americans by creating within us a new consciousness. Black Power-Black Consciousness serves as a defense against the state of non-being and a racist society.

We are even protected against White supremacy, a satanic global movement that seeks to destroy people of color. Black Power-Black Consciousness is a *social corrective* in combating the forces of local and global racism.

According to Webster, racism "is the assumption that psychocultural traits and capacities are determined by biological race and that races differ decisively from one another which is visually coupled with a belief in the inherent superiority of a particular race for its rights to dominance."[3] African American Liberation Theology supports James Cone's insistence that Black Power-Black Consciousness is an affirmation of the humanity of Blacks in spite of White racism.[4] Cone and I both agree that through Christ, power is bestowed upon Blacks. We also agree that the goal of Black Power-Black Consciousness is a self-determining people. The goal of this God given gift is nothing less than "full participation in the decision making processes affecting the lives of Black people."[5]

African Americans who struggle to obtain liberation on North American soil often suffer from an unspoken fear of genocide implemented by White supremacists. White supremacy is a form of insanity and sin sickness. Europeans have spread this infectious disease throughout the entire continent of Africa.

African Americans are the product of that social disease. However, what man meant for evil, God means for good. Given our strategic placement in North America, the African American community has a special role to play in the 21st century. With the assistance of almighty God, African Americans will not only achieve liberation but we will demonstrate God's greatness to the world.

We are the strongest, fittest survivors of the African Diaspora. We understand firsthand the negative ramifications of the inhumane, violent, barbaric scattering of the African family and its evil purpose—the creation of the African slave. Thus, the stand begins here, in America, with us—God's choice from the many tribes taken during the slave trade and African colonization.

Black Power-Black Consciousness is a powerful spiritual weapon that has and will serve as an effective defense against the satanic and carnal forces of White supremacy. Principalities and powers cannot stand against Divine Black Power. This God-given power has surfaced during critical times throughout our history. It has interfered with White society's failed attempt to force us into a state of non-being. Most important, there can be no thought of liberation for African Americans without this power and consciousness.

Black Power-Black Consciousness has stood against White hatred and Black self-hatred. It has successfully stood against the White perpetrators of evil on the earth.

James Cone believes that Black Power is "an attitude, an inward affirmation of the essential worth of blackness...Black Power is the power of the Black man to say Yes to his own 'black being,' and to make others accept him or be prepared for a struggle."[6]

However, African American Liberation Theology insists that Black Power-Black Consciousness is a product of God, the source of all power. Black Power was created by God for African Americans in their quest for liberation. The supporting scripture for this assessment can be found in Romans 8:31: "What shall we then say to these things If God be for us, who can be against us?"

The Seven Aspects of Black Power-Black Consciousness

Earlier we identified the seven aspects of Black Power-Black Consciousness that I believe are critical to the quest for liberation. These seven aspects will also help us understand the early impetuous demonstrations of Black Power during the 1960s. African American Liberation Theology seeks to shape this raw power by acknowledging its source (almighty God) and applying Christian principles to create discipleship and instill emotional discipline.

1. Black Power-Black Consciousness is an affirmation of our inalienable African humanity. The Rodney King police brutality case questioned the humanity of African Americans. However, the arrogant White perpetrators of this incident unexpectedly collided against Black Power-Black Consciousness. King, who was almost beaten to death by White officers, was captured on film, yet a Simi Valley jury returned an alarming verdict.[7] This jury viewed King as an animal that struck fear in the hearts of several heavily armed White police officers. Since

King was an animal, the beating was justified. Indeed, animals are treated with more kindness that King was.[8]

The atrocity perpetrated against Latasha Harlins was also captured on film. A female Korean merchant shot Harlins in back of the head.[9] The two incidents were the culmination of a long, sordid relationship between the LAPD and the African American community. A riot was ignited in L.A. in 1992. This insurrection was a wake-up call to the powers that be. African Americans proclaimed that we have human rights that must and will be respected.

Riots are the reaction of an oppressed people who have been subjected much too long to economic deprivation. These explosive, violent, impromptu eruptions were raw forms of Black Power-Black Consciousness. Black Power-Black Consciousness stood against the long night of the slavocracy. It was an idea whose time had come.

2. Black Power-Black Consciousness is a social corrective designed to combat the forces of racism. Police brutality against approximately 75 African Americans at a speakeasy sparked the Detroit Riot of 1967. In 1965, the Watts Riot in Los Angeles exploded when a White police officer used excessive force while arresting a Black man during an alleged drunk driving incident. The Chicago Riot of 1919 was the direct result of the refusal of White police to apprehend the White men who stoned to death an innocent Black boy whose only crime was that he swam in Lake Michigan. The Houston Riot of 1917 was instigated by a

White police officer who brutalized a Black soldier who heroically came to the aid of a Black woman.[10]

Riots were early demonstrations of Black Power-Black Consciousness, and they opened the door for a more mature, disciplined expression. The mental chains that once imprisoned the minds, hearts, and souls of African Americans begin to dissolve under the power of the Holy Spirit. The chains were replaced with self-determined spiritual agendas.

Black Power-Black Consciousness progressed to another level of maturity with the Brown vs. Board of Education victory. This legal decision serves as an excellent example of how one individual struggle for equality and liberation can create ripples throughout the entire Black race. Black Power-Black Consciousness boldly knocked on the door of the Supreme Court as George E. C. Hayes, Thurgood Marshall, and James M. Nabrit, Jr. argued the landmark case against segregation.[11]

3. Black Power-Black Consciousness is a defense against the state of non-being. The brush fire of Black Power-Black Consciousness continued to spread and evolve as CORE (Congress of Racial Equality) launched a second attempt to end segregation on the interstate buses and trains; the previous attempt in 1940 failed but with a new surge of Black Consciousness, nonviolent protest prompted a second try under the campaign of the Freedom Riders in 1961.[12] Their nonviolent stand was challenged by Birmingham police commissioner Eugene Bull Conner. Conner encouraged the beating, often into unconsciousness, of

Blacks and Whites. More than 300 buses ventured to the deep South and were met with brutality.[13]

Lunch counter protests in the South gained momentum and spread to more than half a dozen cities. James Lawson, a pacifist who spent time in India with Mahatma Gandhi, endorsed the use of nonviolent protest as a primary tool against the shackles of oppression. Lawson and other leaders believed that "segregation had to be fought on a case-by-case basis, and each racist institution had to be attacked separately."[14]

The spirit of freedom and equality promoted by the Black Power-Black Consciousness movement spread to every sector of the Black church. This special God given consciousness infused the seven historic Black denominations, including the African Methodist Episcopal (A.M.E.) Church; the African Methodist Episcopal Zion Church; the Christian Methodist Episcopal; the National Baptist Convention, U.S.A., Incorporated; the National Baptist Convention of America, Unincorporated; the Progressive National Baptist Convention; and the Church Of God In Christ (C.O.G.I.C.)[15]

4. Black Power-Black Consciousness is a weapon in the quest for African American liberation. Soul Theology is another form of Black Power-Black Consciousness. This theology supported the notion that historically, the Black race had soul sisters and soul brothers in the realm of the spirit that could assist them in the tedious quest for temporal empowerment.

Soul Theology emerged as Black activists and artists introduced the Black Virgin Mary and the Black Baby Jesus. The concept of a Black Messiah was popularized in the late 1960s and early 1970s by Rev. Albert Cleage's Shrine of the Black Madonna in Detroit, Michigan. Cleage's *Black Power Theology* preceded Cone's Black Liberation Theology. Black Power Theology's creed proclaimed that the human family began in Africa millions of years ago. God, who was "a combination of black, yellow and red with just a little touch of White," presented a Black Son to the world in the person of Jesus.[16]

Collectively and individually, Blacks began to claim the biblical promise of freedom and deliverance. Blackness was perceived "as a special creation of God," and as recipients of this gift, we no longer needed to be ashamed of this attribute but could be reborn into a positive Black identity."[17]

Black Consciousness began to positively affect the church as well as the secular arena. The invigorated Black church became exactly what almighty God wanted it to be—a "soulful community-based organization with the potential for generating collective power. Revitalized and rooted in an Afro-centric theology of liberation, the church would serve as a spiritual helpmeet, custodian of the African American cultural heritage, and chief promoter of the empowering doctrine."[18]

In the secular realm, a militant Black Consciousness was born and gained popularity among younger, impatient Blacks. CORE and other organizations became a force to be reckoned with during the Black Power Era.

CORE was founded in Chicago during World War II. This previously nonviolent, direct-action protest organization underwent a major change in ideology as the national director, James Farmer, was replaced in the late 1960s by Floyd McKissick. Under the leadership of McKissick, White supporters were excused and delegates unanimously embraced the Black Power slogan, thus dissolving their long time union with the nonviolent movement. The word "multiracial" was dropped from the constitution in1967 and, before long, the national director could be heard talking about Blacks living as a "nation within a nation."[19] Roy Innis, his successor, proclaimed that separation was indeed CORE's ultimate goal.[20]

5. *Black Power-Black Consciousness is a catalyst that stimulates positive self-identity.* From 1965 to 1975, the separatist ideology was entertained by many visionaries. During the Great Depression, Elijah Muhammad introduced the idea of an Asian Black Nation. Muhammad declared that all African Americans of the African Diaspora were members of this nation, the great tribe of Shabazz.[21] Integrating with our 400-year-old enemy was out of the question. Peace could only be achieved by separating the races. Freedom for African Americans would come when every man and woman, Black and White, returned to their countries of origin.

The mental poisoning caused by the former slave master would dissolve when the races separated. Muhammad believed that whether the territorial separation took place in North America or not, the U.S. government was obliged to finance and maintain for at least twenty-five years the expatriate settlement. Muhammad said that it was "far more important to teach separation of the Blacks and Whites in America than prayer."[22]

6. Black Power-Black Consciousness is a defense against genocide. The Republic of New Africa (RNA) was formed during the 1960s by Milton Henry, a Yale educated Detroit lawyer, and his brother Richard. After joining Malcolm X in Detroit, they dropped their slave names and became Brother Gaidi Obadele and Imari Abubakari Obadele, respectively.

The call for partial compensation and five Southern states (to be formed into a new Black Nation) would come by way of government reparation for the long centuries of injustice and slavery imposed upon Blacks. The states of Louisiana, Mississippi, Alabama, Georgia, and South Carolina would constitute the subjugated territory. Ujamaa (cooperative economics) would guide the development of the New Republic's economy.

If the government lacked enthusiasm and was not willing to bargain with the officers of the Republic, an official organized army, the New African Security Force, would be ready for civil war. In this war, the water would be poisoned, gasoline would be destroyed, and not one single bridge would be left standing in the Southern region of the United States, the site of the proposed battle. The RNA also planned to employ urban guerrillas throughout the urban North. The goal was to divide the White U.S. forces and bring Northern industry to the brink of total collapse.[23]

During the late 1960s, the Black Panther Party, a revolutionary nationalist group that subscribed to Black Power-Black Consciousness, received more publicity than any other group. With a core membership of less than a hundred, the Panthers, founded in Oakland, California, in 1966, formed chapters throughout the world. By the 1970s, membership expanded to more than 19 states (35 cities and the District of Columbia).[24]

This youthful, outspoken group supported Eldridge Cleaver's proclamation of "total liberty for black people or total destruction for America."[25] To support this philosophy, the Panthers conducted classes in the expert use of firearms. The leaders insisted that this skill would only be used for self-defense against the unjust attacks of the White enemy.

The Panthers, who saw the police as the enemy of the people, were armed guardians that proudly defended the oppressive social order that enslaved Blacks. Huey P. Newton, the minister of defense, in an effort to inspire revolutionary action, organized ordinary Black people. Liberation schools were established to teach Black youth how to fight against oppression.

7. Black Power-Black Consciousness is a corrective for self-hatred. Maulana Karenga served as a lightning rod for nationalist sentiment by leading a "Back to Black" movement. Karenga inaugurated the celebration of Black holidays, sponsored art events within the Black community, championed the teaching of Swahili, and endorsed Black clothing, hairstyle, and Afrocentric expression. Karenga, the keeper of the tradition, developed the Nguzo Saba (a set of African-based principles) promoting Black Liberation and community. Karenga believed that this approach would create a new people, a new world within the contemporary African American community.[26] The seven principles of the Nguzo Saba are as follows: *Umoja* (unity), *Kujichagulia* (self-determination), *Ujima* (collective work and responsibility), *Ujamaa* (cooperative economics), *Nia* (purpose), *Kuumba* (creativity), and *Imani* (faith).[27]

Kwanzaa was developed as an alternative to the gift giving and economic exploitation of Christmas. This Afrocentric holiday is observed from December 26 to January 1st and was launched in Los Angeles in 1966.[28] The Nguzo Saba and Kwanzaa were powerful expressions of Black Power-Black Consciousness. They supported the ideology and practice of *Kawaida*, "the theory of cultural and social change... which insists that African Americans need to carry out a cultural revolution before they could mount a successful political campaign to seize and reorder, establish institutions of power and wealth. Black liberation was impossible, by definition unthinkable, without breaking the White culture's domination of black minds."[29]

To many proponents of cultural nationalism, Kawaida provided an alternative to acculturation. Newark born and Howard University educated Amiri Baraka, a chief proselytizer of Kawaida, was determined to develop an aesthetic that would separate African Americans from the Euro-Americans.[30] Formerly LeRoi Jones, Baraka wrote numerous essays, plays, and books from 1961 through 1966.

Baraka's nationalist vision included Black dominated city-states, such as Gary, Detroit, Harlem, East St. Louis, and Newark; the transformation of economically depressed colonies ruled by Whites into park-like living areas decorated with neo-African designed homes and shops; and the eventual rise of a World African Party which would unite the African Diaspora. Baraka saw the Nguzo Saba as a key element in creating the new nationalism. He said that "Black art is change, it must force change, it must be change."[31]

African American Liberation Theology is based on the premise that the cultural integrity of African Americans is maintained by separation, while integration promotes spiritual ecumenism. Hope springs not from persecution or crucifixion, but resurrection. Black Power-Black Consciousness cannot exist in the hearts, minds, and souls of African Americans without the resurrection power of God to deliver His chosen from persecution and crucifixion. As Christians we know, Jesus Christ bore the burden of persecution and crucifixion so that we don't have to.

Then the Lord said unto Moses, Now shalt thou see what I will do to Pharaoh: for with a strong hand shall he let them go, and with a strong hand shall he drive them out of this land. And God spake unto Moses, and said unto him, I am the Lord: And I appeared unto Abraham, unto Isaac, and unto Jacob, by the name of God Almighty, but by my name JEHOVAH was I not known to them.

And I have also established my covenant with them, to give them the land of Canaan, the land of their pilgrimage, wherein they were strangers. And I have also heard the groaning of the children of Israel, whom the Egyptians keep in bondage: and I have remembered my covenant. Wherefore say unto the children of Israel, I am the Lord, and I will bring you out from under the burdens of the Egyptians, and I will rid you out of their bondage, and I will redeem you with a stretched out arm, and with great judgements; And I will take you to me for a people, and I will be to you a God: and ye shall know that I am the Lord your God, which bringeth you out from under the burdens of the Egyptians. And I will bring you in unto the land, concerning the which I did swear to give it to Abraham, to Isaac, and to Jacob; and I will give it you for an heritage: I am the Lord.— Exodus 6:1–8

Now upon the first day of the week, very early in the morning, they came unto the sepulchre, bringing the spices which they had prepared, and certain others with them. And they found the stone rolled away from the sepulchre. And they entered in, and found not the body of the Lord Jesus. And it came to pass as they were much perplexed thereabout, behold two men stood by them in shining garments. And as they were afraid, and bowed down their faces to the earth, they said unto them, Why seek ye the living among the dead? He is not here but is risen: remember how he spake unto you when he was yet in Galilee. Saying, the son of man must be delivered into the hands of sinful men, and be crucified, and the third day rise again. And they remembered his words.— Luke 24:1–8

The state of non-being created by White supremacy is maintained by fear. However, with Black Power-Black Consciousness, we have the courage to be. We are not afraid. "For God hath not given us the spirit of fear, but of power, and of love, and of a sound mind" (2 Timothy 1:7).

With Divine Black Power, we are resurrected from a state of non-being. We have the victory over suffering, death, and sin.

Therefore being justified by faith we have peace with God through our Lord Jesus Christ: By whom also we have access by faith into this grace wherein we stand and rejoice in hope of the glory of God. And not only so but we glory in tribulation also, knowing that tribulation worketh patience, and patience experience and experience hope. And hope maketh not ashamed, because the love of God is shed abroad in our hearts by the Holy Ghost which is given us.— Romans 5:1–5

With Black Power-Black Consciousness, African Americans are resurrected with new values and a new spirituality. We can look forward to resurrection beyond death, oppression (political, economic, social), and daily degradation.

Historically, all great movements begin in the consciousness of the people. African American Liberation Theology began in the consciousness of oppressed Blacks and was implemented with Divine Black Power. God has resurrected us from the dead and we are now empowered with life and a positive identity.

Chapter 4: Communal Unification

Through the experienced eyes of my ancestors
I became an unwilling spectator—
to the movement of my people

My cup was running over,
I prayed on behalf of African Americans
I prayed to a power that can do what no other power can do
Indeed, the spirit of the Lord was upon me

Suddenly!
These words were placed upon the tablets of my heart
For thou who rule, the storm and the rain
He promised, to stand by me

With this gesture, the eyes of my soul were opened
I realized that—
Every link in the chain of Slavocracy had been broken
Every link in the chain of the Slave Trade had been broken
Every link in the chain of Segregation had been broken
Every link in the chain of degradation had been broken

My soul could now rest.
We are not the children of a lesser God.[1]

Before we can entertain integration or separatism, before we can attest to the spiritual gift of Black Power-Black Consciousness, before we can receive the blessing of the resurrection, before we can achieve equal and separate, before we can implement our individual and collective spiritual agendas—we must come to terms with the fact that we are indeed God's elect. We have been chosen. Then and only then can the elect move from the state of non-being to receiving Divine Black Power. Once endowed with Divine Black Power, the elect can move courageously toward liberation and resurrection.

Spiritual preparation serves a special purpose. God is not only moving African Americans toward liberation, He is spiritually preparing the elect to do battle against White cultural prodigalism. I'll explain this term in greater depth later in the chapter, but suffice it to say that cultural prodigalism is an advanced form of White racism.

Earlier, I discussed the idea that African Americans have been chosen by God for a special purpose. More precisely, many have been called but few have been chosen. In African American Liberation Theology, there is no such thing as a monolithic African American community. In fact, we must include as part of our liberation strategy the ostracizing of rebellious, sinful, and disobedient African Americans. This hypothesis, I have categorized as the Rule of the Unchosen.

The Bible supports this idea. Witness the story of Noah in the Old Testament Book of Genesis.

But Noah found grace in the eyes of the Lord. These are the generations of Noah: Noah was a just man and perfect in his generations, and Noah walked with God. Moreover, when God determined that all flesh was corrupt upon the earth and filled with violence He spared the family of Noah which included his wife, three sons (Ham, Shem, and Japheth) and their wives.— Genesis 6:8–9

Genesis also gives an account of two brothers, Cain and Abel, the offspring of Adam and Eve. Cain was a farmer, Abel was a sheep herder. The brothers made their offerings to the Lord. The Lord respected Abel's offering, but rejected Cain's. According to Genesis 4: 6-7, God gave special instructions to Cain.

And the Lord said unto Cain why art thou wroth? And why is thy countenance fallen? If thou doest well shalt thou not be accepted? And if thou doest not well, sin lieth at the door. And unto thee shall be his desire, and thou shall rule over him. However, Cain filled with jealously, slew his brother, and God therefore set a mark upon Cain that if anyone find him in the land of his father that he should be killed.

Abel was chosen, Cain, was not.

The call of Abraham and the sparing of Lot's family also provides evidence of God choosing certain men while rejecting others.

Now the Lord had said unto Abram, Get thee out of thy country, and from thy kindred, and from thy father house, unto a land that I will shew thee. And I will make thee a great nation, and I will bless thee, and make thy name great; and thou shalt be a blessing. And I will bless them that bless thee, and curse him that curseth thee: And in thee shall all families of the earth be blessed.— Genesis 12:1–3

When the Lord decided to destroy the sinful cities of Sodom and Gomorrah, Abraham (formerly Abram) asked that Lot be spared if God found him to be righteous, and God complied. Joshua's victory at Jericho exemplifies how God turns away from the sinful or undeserving. When the walls of Jericho fell, God granted special instructions to the victors—to utterly destroy all that was in the city—men, women, children, and animals (Joshua 6:21). Only the prostitute Rahab and her father, mother, and brother avoided the destruction.

The wars of King David offer evidence of God's favor toward certain individuals and groups. When David sought counsel with the Lord before every battle, he would ask for favor over the opposing army. According to 2 Samuel 5:19, David asked for victory over the Philistines. Often, God instructed David, the victor, to spare no one. Those who were not chosen were sentenced to death.

Job was also chosen by God. Job was special to God. There was none like him in the earth. He was a perfect and an upright man, one that feared God, and eschewed evil. Even when God allowed Satan to test him, "still he holdeth fast his integrity, although thou movedst me against him, to destroy him without a cause" (Job 2:3). After the test, God called Satan's terror reign upon Job's life to an end. He not only restored Job's losses but blessed him abundantly.

Scripture definitely supports the idea that God has selected certain African Americans, according to His divine standard and merit of grace, to uplift the race. Unfortunately, many African Americans have consciously chosen to displease God. Through their continuous occupation with lust, disobedience, blood sin, and self-hatred, many have worshipped false gods, including the idols of capitalism and materialism. African Americans have been guilty of adultery, fornication, uncleanliness, lasciviousness, idolatry, witchcraft, hatred, strife, sedition, heresies, envy, murder, and drunkenness. The unchosen is vain, they desire glory, and they walk in the counsel of the ungodly.

According to the first book of Psalm, the ungodly do not delight themselves or meditate in the law of the Lord, but are like chaff which the wind drives away. The way of the ungodly shall perish.

The 37th Psalm of David depicts the fate of the unchosen: "Fret not thyself because of evildoers, neither be thou envious against the workers of iniquity. For they shall soon be cut down like the grass, and wither as the green herb... for evil doers shall be cut off."

Psalm 37:12–15 says,

> The wicked plotted against the just, and gnasheth
> upon him with his teeth. The Lord shall laugh at him: for
> He seeth that his day is coming. The wicked have drawn
> out the sword, and have bent their bow, to cast down the
> poor and needy, and to slay such as be of upright conver-
> sation. Their sword shall enter into their own heart, and
> their bows shall be broken.

Verse 20 seals the fate of the wicked: "But the wicked
shall perish, and the enemies of the Lord shall be as the fat of
lambs: they shall consume; into smoke shall they consume away."

The word of God is clear. Defiant, rebellious African
Americans will receive a deadly blow from the hand of God.
Their seed will be scattered and eventually will completely van-
ish from the face of the earth. Their color will not save them
from God's wrath.

Take the case of the children of Israel who suffered the
tyranny of the Egyptians. Not all of the people who were delivered from Egypt entered the promised land; not all of those who
sojourned with Moses found favor with God.

> And when the people saw that Moses delayed to
> come down out of the mount, the people gathered them-
> selves unto Aaron, and said unto him, Up, make us gods,

which shall go before us; for as for this Moses, the man that brought us up out of the land of Egypt, we know not what is become of him... Aaron therefore built an altar to house the molten (golden) calf. The Lord, seeing the disobedience of His children, declared unto Moses that the people were a stiff-necked people.— Exodus 32:1

Now therefore let me alone, that my wrath may wax hot against them, and that I may consume them: And I will make of thee a great nation.— Exodus 32:10

Then Moses stood in the gate of the camp, and saith, Who is on the Lord's side? Let him come unto me. And all the sons of Levi gathered together unto him.— Exodus 32: 26

And the Lord said unto Moses, Whosoever hath sinned against me, him will I blot out of my book.— Exodus 32:33

And the Lord plagued the people, because they made the calf, which Aaron made.— Exodus 32:35

After those who had sinned were destroyed, God gave specific instructions (pertaining to the possessing of the land) to the chosen.

And the Lord spake unto Moses in the plains of Moab by Jordan near Jericho, saying, Speak unto the children of Israel, and say unto them, When ye are passed over Jordan into the land of Canaan. Then ye shall drive out all the inhabitants of the land from before you, and destroy all their pictures, and destroy all their molten images, and quite pluck down all their high places: And ye shall dispossess the inhabitants of the land, and dwell therein: for I have given you the land to possess it.— Numbers 33:50–53

Not all African Americans who were delivered out of the slavocracy will share in the fruits of America—the new Promised Land. Neither their color nor their membership in an oppressed group will save them if they have been disobedient and sinful.

From the ashes of our historical chaos and cultural tribulations, God is preparing a nation of the African American elect. Some believe that all African Americans have been chosen by God because of our suffering and Black lineage. This idea is not scripturally based. Romans 9:6–11 says,

Not as though the word of God hath taken none effect, For they are not all Israel, which are of Israel: Neither, because they are the seed of Abraham, are they all children: but, in Isaac shall thy seed be called. That is, they which are the children of the flesh, these are not the children of God: but the children of the promise are counted for the seed. For this is the word of promise, At this time will I come, and Sarah shall have a son. And not only this; but when Rebecca also had conceived by one, even by our Father Isaac; (For the children being not yet born, neither having done any good or evil, that the purpose of God according to election might stand, not of works, but of him that calleth.)

Remember, African Americans are the products of God's divine selection. We, the pluralistic mix of Africans in the Diaspora, represent the survival of the fittest. These select Africans, under the power of the Holy Spirit, are transformed into new creatures, from beasts of burden to suffering servants, from slaves to ex-slaves, from Negroes to African Americans. We will escape the tyranny of slavocracy and experience the triumph of liberation. Africans and other oppressed people throughout the world who have been chosen by God will form an ecumenical family, tied by agape love and the bloodline of humanity.

Through African Americans, the world will see what God can do. We, who were homeless, enslaved, and raped, have been chosen to demonstrate God's mercy and grace. Through His omnipotent power, God excavated the seed of those Africans who were crossbred to near extinction and summoned forth a new Black race. We are like the army of soldiers God resurrected from the ashes and bones of the dead. According to Ezekiel 37:1–14,

The hand of the Lord was upon me, and carried me out in the spirit of the Lord, and set me down in the midst of the valley which was full of bones, And caused me to pass by them round about: and, behold, there were very many in the open valley; and, lo, they were very dry. And he said unto me, Son of man, can these bones live? And I answered, O Lord God, thou knowest. Again he said unto me, Prophesy upon these bones, and say unto them, O ye dry bones, hear the word of the Lord. Thus saith the Lord God unto these bones; Behold, I will cause breath to enter into you, and ye shall live: And I will lay sinews upon you, and will bring up flesh upon you, and cover you with skin, and put breath in you, and ye shall live; and ye shall know that I am the Lord. So I prophesied as I was commanded: and as I prophesied, there was a noise, and behold a shaking, and the bones came together, bone to his bone. And when I beheld, lo, the sinews and the flesh came up upon them, and the skin covered them above: but there was no breath in them.

Then saith he unto me, Prophesy unto the wind, prophesy, son of man, and say to the wind, thus saith the Lord God; Come from the four winds, O breathe, and breath, and breathe upon these slain, that they may live. So I prophesied as he commanded me, and the breath came into them, and they lived, and stood up upon their feet, an exceeding great army. Then he said unto me,

Son of man, these bones are the whole house of Israel: behold, they say, Our bones are dried, and our hope is lost: we are cut off for our parts. Therefore prophesy and say unto them, Thus said the Lord God: Behold, O my people, I will open your graves, and cause you to come up out of your graves, and bring you into the land of Israel. And ye shall know that I am the Lord, when I have opened your graves, O my people, and brought you up out of your graves. And shall put my spirit in you, and ye shall live, and I shall place you in your own land: then shall ye know that I the Lord have spoken it, and performed it, saith the Lord.

This resurrection initiated by God would set the stage for global liberation and encourage the oppressed throughout the world to strive for freedom. African Americans who were summoned from the Valley of Dry Bones by the voice of God (during the long night of slavery) would stand on their feet and demand their freedom. Summoned by the voice of God, African Americans acquired their citizenship while at the bottom of the social ladder.

Due to our increasing involvement in political, educational, and economic arenas we have the advantage over other oppressed people of color. We have the political base necessary to influence the policies of tyrannical governments. Notwithstanding our struggle for equality and a more egalitarian society continue to this very day. We are still the most capable members of the African Diaspora. We are strategically positioned to declare a new Emancipation Proclamation, Reconstruction, and civil rights era. We are a force to be reckoned with.

Africans and other people of color have been elected to join the ranks of the chosen. African Americans will assist others who have been chosen. African Americans are the best of what mother Africa had to offer and the strongest from each tribe. As the strongest, we were created into a new people who could stand against degradation and demand equality and liberation. According to Dwight N. Hopkins, author of *Introducing Black Theology of Liberation*, African Americans are remnants of God's purpose on earth who must essentially, "bear the burdens of taking the lead and changing America into what God has created all mankind to become."[2]

Persecution, Crucifixion, Resurrection

Persecution, crucifixion, and resurrection were the process of salvation and deliverance depicted in both the Old Testament stories of the children of Israel and the New Testament centerpiece, the life and passion of Jesus Christ.

In the Book of Exodus, a new king determined that the children of Israel were growing too rapidly. As a result, he decided to enslave them to lessen the chances of an allegiance with the enemies of Egypt. This enslavement represents the persecution.

The building of Pharaoh's treasure cities, Pithum and Raamses, became the slaves' task. Despite their enslavement, the children of Israel continued to multiply and grow. The mid-wives were instructed to kill all males at birth, and Pharaoh instructed the people to cast every male born Hebrew child into the river. This represents the crucifixion.

Moses was called by God to deliver his people out of bondage. God unleashed a series of deadly plagues to force Pharaoh's hand. After the tenth plague (the death of the first-born), Pharaoh was persuaded to free the children of Israel. They followed Moses into the wilderness. It was there that they received the Ten Commandments and entered into an eternal covenant with God. This represents the resurrection.

In the New Testament, we witness the same process of persecution, crucifixion, and resurrection in the life of Jesus the Christ. Jesus was persecuted by many. Due to the social tension his ministry and presence generated, the Son of God was delivered to Pontious Pilate and the Roman government. This blameless man, the Son of the Living God, was treated as a criminal and stood trial for conspiracy and insurrection against the reigning government. This was Jesus' persecution.

The crucifixion of Christ was ordered by the chief priest, rulers, and the people. The crucifixion took place at Calvary. Jesus was even made to carry the cross that He would be nailed to.

The resurrection followed three days later, and it was Mary Magdalene who proclaimed to the disciples that Christ had risen from the grave.

There are modern day examples of the process of salvation and deliverance. The Jews went through the process. For centuries, the Jewish people suffered antisemitism because of the assumption that they murdered Christ and that they were tools of the devil. This was their the persecution.

The murder of about six million Jews was perpetrated by Adolph Hitler's Nazi Germany during World War II. And while Slavs, Gypsies, and political dissidents were targeted, only the Jews were selected for total annihilation.[3] Adolph Hitler believed that the Jews "were carriers of a genetic inheritance that mortally threatened German and Christian values."[4] It was this distorted perception that inevitably fueled the hatred that caused the great pain and suffering of the Jews of Germany as well as the bulk of European Jewry.

The Jews suffered their crucifixion at the death camps of Auschwitz, Dachau, and Buchenwald in Germany, Chelmno, Majdenek, and Treblinka in Poland.[5] "Upon arrival, about one tenth were used as slave labor until murdered. Others were killed immediately in gas chambers disguised as showers. Their bodies were cremated after their gold teeth, hair, and clothes were taken for the German war effort."[6]

The resurrection of the Jews finally came on September 2, 1945, with a formal surrender by the government of Japan.[7] With the death of Hitler and the surrender of the Berlin garrison on May 2, the Jews reported the inhumane atrocities of the Nazi war criminals. Jews now enjoy a well-deserved freedom of religious expression (especially in the United States). They even have their own homeland in the Middle East.

This process of salvation and deliverance is also manifest in the Black experience. The persecution came about through African enslavement. Millions of our ancestors died during the ocean passage from Africa to the Americas and Europe and during slavery itself. This was our persecution and crucifixion.

But what of our resurrection? It is still occurring, but thank God it began with the end of the Civil War and gained momentum during the civil rights movement.

The resurrection is a weeding out process. It sorts through the elect who submit to God's will and those who are disobedient. The unchosen will be consumed by their own lust, hatred, and disobedience. The elect will bear fruit and their offspring will continue to resurrect and become vital human instruments in the implementation of African American Liberation Theology.

We are a people in transition. We have endured persecution and crucifixion, but thank God, we are now at the resurrection phase of the cycle. God has heard our cry, so let not your heart be troubled. Throughout history, God has never, nor will He ever, let evil win. Evil, which corrodes our communities from within, is presently on a collision course with God. God is never defeated; God never retreats.

With God's help, a race of strong, productive African Americans will establish a new legacy for ourselves and future generations. God is using African American Liberation Theology to call a select few to give new meaning to the Gospel of Jesus Christ and Old Testament messages of liberation.

Cultural Prodigalism

Earlier in this chapter, I mentioned that cultural prodigalism is an extreme form of White racism. Allow me to explain. Cultural prodigalism, which is essential in understanding African American Liberation Theology, describes the environmental destruction and human injustice unleashed by Whites upon the world. This theory is named after the biblical story of the prodigal son (Luke 15:11–24):

> A certain man had two sons. And the younger of them said to his father, father, give me the share of the property that falls to me. And he divided his means between them. And not many days later, the younger son gathered up all his wealth, and took his journey into a far country; and there he squandered his fortune in loose living. And after he had spent all, there came a grievous famine over that country, and he began himself to suffer want. And he went and joined one of the citizens of that country, who sent him to his farm to feed swine. And he longed to fill himself with the pods that the swine were eating, but no one offered to give them to him. But when he came to himself, he said, 'How many hired men in my

father's house have bread in abundance, while I am per-ishing here with hunger! I will get up and go to my father, and will say to him, Father, I have sinned against heaven and before thee. I am no longer worthy to be called thy son; make me as one of the hired men.' And he arose and went to his father. But while he was yet a long way off, his father saw him and was moved with compassion, and ran and fell upon his neck and kissed him. And the son said to him, 'Father, I have sinned against heaven and before thee. I am no longer worthy to be called thy son.' But the father said to his servants, 'fetch quickly the best robe and put it on him, and give him a ring for his finger and sandals for his feet; and bring out the fattened calf and kill it, and let us eat and make merry; because my son was dead, and has come to life again; he was lost, and is found.' And they began to make merry.

This story relates not only to the enslavement of African Americans and acts of genocide, but also to the exploitation of the world's natural resources by the White race—resources which God intended to be used by the entire human family. This social phenomenon is a by-product of Original Sin, the sin of all sins. Original Sin was set in motion by Adam and Eve. It separated us from God and our sisters and brothers.

Until the Prodigal Race (i.e., the White race), return to the human family in atonement, the wrath of God shall be upon their children and their children's children. Specifically, the term "White race" refers to White Europeans, their ancestors (the founders of the thirteen American colonies and colonizers of Africa), and their descendants. God will unleash natural disasters, diseases, and plagues on the heads of the Prodigal Race until it repents and turns from its wicked ways. The Prodigal Race must ask God, the heavenly Father, for forgiveness.

White supremacy has caused many races to literally disappear from the face of the earth. For example, the Kohi-San people of South Africa were viciously exterminated; small, scattered remnants of Australia's Aborigines find themselves in a situation similar to the North American Native Indians. In the Belgian Congo during the last two decades of the 19th century, it is estimated that eight to twelve million Africans died. Similarly, the Amerindians of Central and South America were decimated; the Arwaks and Caribs of the Caribbean no longer exist.[8] Since Columbus' invasion, it is estimated that there were about 112,554,000 indigenous people living in the Western Hemisphere. In 1980, the stunning total was only 28,264,000.[9]

There is an unspoken fear among African Americans that former slave masters will attempt to perpetrate genocide. Indigenous people on seven continents also have this fear.[10]

Since we intimately know White supremacy, I believe that God has given us the holy mission of defeating it. The African American community has a special role to play during the 21st century. Not only must we educate ourselves about domestic affairs, we must become intelligent about the course of events throughout the world, particularly in Africa, Europe, and Asia. "The struggle between Europe and Asia to conquer the world, with global Black people as the battlefield, is by far our greatest challenge."[11]

Evidence of cultural prodigalism can be found in how the world's natural resources have been exploited and how indigenous communities have been destabilized through global colonialism. For example, U.S. residents only represent about five percent of the world's population, we consume about 60 percent of the world's energy resources.[12] White men from Europe and the United States, as well as men from other class and racial elites from other countries, are our primary concern. "A radical analysis of the state of environmental affairs requires understanding that this class, race, and gender profile is neither coincidental nor inconsequential."[13]

The gatekeepers of capitalist, socialist, and monarchist states share a common denominator, i.e., the hegemony of privileged White masculinity. This usually transcends national allegiances or political ideology. The exploitation of precious rainforests in Myanar (formerly Burma), Thailand, and Malaysia are a direct result of cooperative ventures connecting industry, governments, and military interests.

Another major example of cultural prodigalism can be found in the destruction and displacement of indigenous people. The World Bank and International Monetary Fund has virtually enslaved developing nations around the world. With extremely high interest rates, payback is, not surprisingly, virtually impossible to accomplish. In a desperate effort to payback loans and save face, indigenous landowners are often forced to abandon their land rights. In Indonesia, one million hectares of Indonesia's tropical forest are destroyed per year to pay off a $40 billion debt.[14]

In West Papua, the Moi people are starving due to the uncontested decimation of the forest by timber companies.[15] White cultural prodigalism has led to the dumping of toxic waste (from the United States) into "Third World" countries (who is first and second and why?), thus continuing previous patterns of racism, colonialism, and imperialism. It has become common practice to test nuclear weapons on indigenous people—especially Islanders in the South Pacific.[16] Moreover, the entire island population has been systematically dislocated as many sites became uninhabitable and will remain so for tens of thousands of years. Needless to say, the physical and psychological health consequences are incalculable.

In America, cultural prodigalism leads to the same catastrophic consequences, especially for non-Whites. Since 1963, the United States government has exploded more than 651 nuclear weapons on Native American lands near the western Shoshone territory near Nevada. African American and Latin American communities have some of the nation's largest and most hazardous landfills. These sites account for more than 40 percent of the entire nation's population.[17]

The Southeast side of Chicago, a predominately African American and Latin community, houses the nation's largest concentration of hazardous waste sites in the United States. In the West, Cree communities have witnessed the effects of Manitoba Hydroelectric Dams built during the early 1970s. The system, located between the Nelson and Churchill River Systems, drains one of North America's largest watersheds, causing silt to choke reservoirs, thus destroying wildlife and causing mercury contamination. The people misplaced by this intrusion suffer substance abuse, suicide epidemics, and other severe psychological problems.[18]

Due to the onslaught of White cultural prodigalism on the world, many indigenous governmental and economic systems have been disrupted and destroyed. The Jewish Holocaust stands as a vivid reminder that so-called White supremacy (i.e., cultural prodigalism) must be confronted by all of God's elect. History teaches that this evil, sinful force is capable of irreparable annihilation (upon humans and the ecosystem of the earth).

During the so-called Cold War of 1945–1990, the three major players—the United States, Soviet Union, and Great Britain—possessed considerable resources in comparison to the indigenous states decimated around the world.[19] Recently, trade agreements such as the Canada-United States Free Trade Agreement (CUSTA), the North American Free Trade Agreement (NAFTA), and the General Agreement on Tariffs and Trade (GATT), are enabling global corporations to not only strengthen their control of the world economy but also to rewrite the rules of international trade.[20] This new form of colonialism is nothing more than cultural prodigalism.

In his book *Race, Religion, and Racism,* Fredrick K. C. Price quotes Dr. Anderson: "It is one group's use of wealth and power and resources to deprive, hurt, injure, and exploit another group to benefit itself."[21] Dr. Anderson believes that this intensified racism (cultural prodigalism) actually began in the 16th century when White nations initially began to enslave African people. There is not one recorded instance in history where Blacks have exploited, enslaved, or denied Whites of their basic human rights.[22] However, it is now a matter of record that Whites have used their position of power to maim, kill, exclude, and marginalize Blacks throughout the world.[23]

Clearly, Black Power-Black Consciousness must mature beyond the parameters of the indigenous African American community. It must grow to encompass the collective and individual spiritual agendas of African Americans chosen by God. We are the chosen, and we have been strategically placed in America by God. Those chosen by God will take part in His overall plan to implement global liberation. This unique relationship with God is epic in nature. Its global and indigenous importance is unprecedented.

Currently, cultural prodigalism threatens the existence of African Americans and the entire human family. The God of the oppressed is indeed concerned with social justice for African Americans and oppressed people of color throughout the world.

Indeed, African Americans have been selected as God's chosen people to end the violent injustices perpetrated against the people of the African Diaspora. We have been strategically, purposely placed in the richest, most powerful country in the world. This special inherent blessing issued by God upon the sons and daughters of God must be recognized not only in the great by-and-by but in the here-and-now as well.[24]

African Americans must address, confront, and defeat cultural prodigalism. Our human inheritance (bestowed upon us by God) hangs in the balance.

Dr. King and Malcolm X envisioned a new society in North America. Dr. King called for a restructuring and redistribution of wealth. In searching for a political and economic system that would support the goals and aspirations of African Americans, he concluded that America "had much to learn from Scandinavia's democratic socialist tradition."[25] Dr. King declared that America should move toward the immediate implementation of democratic socialism.

Dr. King warned the privileged minority class of the earth that "there existed no shelter on the planet where they could go and hide from the rising storm of the world's poor. It was impossible to hide as the global poor struggled against unjust systems and attempted to usher in a new moral vision of equal social relations."[26]

Malcolm also leaned toward socialism as a remedy for White supremacy, racism, and capitalism. During his foreign travels, Malcolm observed how socialism preserved the cultures of people of color while abolishing human exploitation.[27] Socialism offered African Americans the freedom and humanity they were denied in capitalistic systems.

Final Word: The Blessings of Blackness

Our first and best line of defense against evil is our Christian faith, combined with the gift of Black Power-Black Consciousness. In this chapter, I'll add the most important gift: Black Love.

Without the spiritual, moral armor of Black Love, the attempt to liberate ourselves will be meaningless—empty intellectualism, empty activism, empty prayers. Without Black Love, African Americans are defenseless and naked. Malcolm was right when he said that the worse crime a race can commit is to teach another race to hate the human image (i.e., African characteristics) that God bestowed upon them.[1] He believed that African Americans must embrace a healthy self-love for the African side of their cultural reality. This, he insisted, we must do first. To attempt to love someone else without first loving self will prove impossible and self-defeating.[2]

Love creates a metamorphosis within us. It spiritually develops our ability to relate to self and others—the church, the community, and nature.[3] Black Love is a weapon against the forces of cultural prodigalism (e.g., capitalism) and the three evils (suffering, death, and sin). Black Love enables us to:

- Receive the gift of Black Consciousness.[4]
- Dismantle the psychological indoctrination of self-hate.[5]
- Receive the God-given right of cultural self-identity and self-determination.[6]
- Defend ourselves against the psychological residue of Willie Lynch indoctrination.[7]

119

- Eliminate the psychological need to imitate European and American culture.[8]
- Remember our original state of Blackness.
- Strengthen the cultural and historic bonds of Africans scattered throughout the Diaspora.[9]

In loving ourselves, we are in essence, loving the Creator who made us in His own image. Within the context of Black Theology, God's love is our Creator's love for the least of society. This love works on a spiritual and carnal plane to bring about each person's full humanity. The ongoing movement of God's spirit, living in the presence of Jesus Christ and manifesting in the Black Experience is a calling, "from a spirit greater than oneself."[10]

Black Love demands that we maintain our culture, community, and church. Our ability to integrate or separate without entering a state of non-being strengthens Black Love. This may not be an easy state for the African American elect to maintain in the face of Black *and* White violence and hatred. However, through the liberating message of African American Liberation Theology, Black Love is clearly an idea whose time has come.

Deep in my heart
I do believe
We will
We must
And we shall overcome.

Black Theology, Black Power & Black Love

1   Martin Luther King Jr., Stride Toward Freedom: The Montgomery Story, p. 43.

2   Ibid., p. 51.

3   Ibid., p. 63.

4   Ibid., p. 170.

5   James Cone, Martin & Malcolm, & America: A Dream or a Nightmare, p. 127.

6   Ibid.

7   Ibid.

8.   King, p. 103.

9   Ibid.

10   Ibid., p. 101.

11   Cone, pp. 129–130.

12   Ibid.

13   Ervin Smith, The Ethics of Martin Luther King, Jr., p. 126.

14   King, pp. 104–107.

15   Cone, p. 122.

16   Ibid., p. 137.

17   Ibid., pp. 137–138.

18   Ibid., p. 137.

19   Ibid., pp. 60–61.

20   Hanes Walton, Jr., The Political Philosophies of Martin Luther King, Jr., p. 30.

21   Ibid., pp. 66–67.

22   Cone, p. 66.

23   Ibid.

24   Ibid., pp. 66–67.

25   Ibid., p. 68.

26   Ibid.

27   Ibid., p. 71.

28   Ibid., p. 69.

29   King, p. 33.

30   Cone, p. 78.

Footnotes- Part 1
Chapter 2

1   James Cone, Martin & Malcolm, & America: A Dream or a Nightmare, p. 107.

2   Ibid., p. 4.

3   George Breitman, The Last Year of Malcolm X—The Evolution of a Revolution, p. 57.

4   Peter Goldman, The Death and Life of Malcolm X, pp. 35–41.

5   Cone, p. 4.

6   Ibid., p. 96.

7   Ibid., p. 15.

8   Ibid.

9   Ibid.

10   Ibid., p. 47.

11   Malcolm X (edited by Imam Benjamin Karim) The End of White World Supremacy: Four Speeches by Malcolm X, pp. 85–94.

12   Cone, p. 39.

13   Ibid., p. 55.

14   Ibid., p. 47.

15   Ibid., pp. 49–54.

16   Ibid., p. 93.

17   Ibid., p. 95.

18   Ibid.

19   Ibid., pp. 95–96.

20   Ibid., p. 95.

21   Ibid., p. 96.

22   Ibid., pp. 96–97.

23   Ibid., p. 97.

24   Ibid.

25   Ibid., pp. 105–110.

26   Ibid.

27   Ibid., p. 107.

28   Breitman, pp. 106–107.

29   Cone, p. 108.

30   Ibid., p. 109.

31   Ibid.

32   Ibid.

33   Ibid., p. 110.

Footnotes- Part 1

Chapter 3

1   Jawanza Kunjufu, Countering the Conspiracy to Destroy Black Boys, p. 1.

2   James Cone, For My People: Black Theology and the Black Church, p. 6.

3   Ibid., p. 7.

4   Ibid., p. 8.

5   Ibid., pp. 8–11.

6   James Cone, Martin & Malcolm, & America—A Dream or a Nightmare, p. 227.

7   James Cone, Black Theology & Black Power, p. 38–39.

8   Ibid., p. 6.

9   Ibid., p. 7.

10 Cone, Martin & Malcolm, & America, p. 288.

11 Cone, For My People, p. 5.

12 Cone, p. 11.

13 Ibid.

14 Cone, Black Theology and Black Power, p. 52.

15 Ibid., p. 53.

16 Ibid., p. 31.

17 Ibid.

18 Ibid., p. 32.

19 Ibid., p. 33.

20 Peter Kreeft, Making Sense Out of Suffering, p. 29.

21 Cone, Black Theology & Black Power, pp. 15–16.

22 Ibid., p. 116.

23   Ibid., p. 117.

24   Ibid., p. 116.

25   Kreeft, p. 24.

26   Cone, Black Theology & Black Power, pp. 125–126.

27   Ibid., pp. 58–59 & 124–125.

28   Ibid., pp. 58–59.

29   Kreeft, p. 69.

30   J. Christiaan Beker, Suffering and Hope, pp. 62–63.

31   Ibid., p. 77.

32   Ibid.

33   Ibid., p. 69.

34   Ibid., p. 58.

35   Paul A. Feider, The Christian Search for Meaning in
        Suffering, p. 10.

36   Cone, Black Theology and Black Power, pp. 58–59.

37   Ibid., p. 59.

38   Ladislaus Boros, Pain and Providence, p. 14.

39   Ibid., pp. 13–14.

40   Cone, Black Theology & Black Power, p. 123.

41   Ibid., p. 126.

42   Ibid.

43   Dr. Martin L. King, Stride Toward Freedom: The
        Montgomery Story, p. 36.

44   Cone, Black Theology & Black Power, p. 28.

45   Ibid., p. 129.

46   Ibid., p. 132.

47   Kreeft, p. 112.

48   Beker, p. 63.

49   Cone, Black Theology & Black Power, p. 132.

Footnotes- Part 2
Chapter 1

1   James Cone, Black Theology & Black Power, p. 16.
2   Ibid., p. 57.
3   Ibid.
4   Ibid., p. 39.
5   Ibid., p. 38.
6   Ibid., p. 37.
7   Ibid., p. 31.

Footnotes- Part II
Chapter 2

1   Toward a Political Hermeneutics of the Gospel, Union Seminary Quarterly Review, pp. 313–314.
2   Fredrick K. C. Price, Race, Religion, and Racism, p. 161.
3   Ibid., p. 169.
4   James Cone, Black Theology & Black Power, p. 35.
5   Ibid., p. 38.
6   Ibid., p. 22.
7   Ibid.
8   Price, p. 171.
9   Dwight N. Hopkins, Shoes That Fit Our Feet, p. 198.
10   Ibid., p. 199.
11   Dwight N. Hopkins, Introducing Black Theology of Liberation, p. 62.
12   Ibid., p. 56.

13   Ibid., p. 73.

14   Ibid.

15   Hopkins, Shoes That Fit Our Feet, p. 200.

16   Ibid.

17   Ibid.

18   Ibid.

19   Ibid., p. 206.

Footnotes- Part II
Chapter 3

1   Cumus, The Rebel, *trans*, Anthony Bower, p. 13.

2   William L. Van Deburg, New Day in Babylon: The Black Power Movement and American Culture, 1965–1975, pp. 176–179.

3   Webster's Dictionary, "Racism," p. 603.

4   James Cone, Black Theology & Black Power, p. 16.

5   Ibid.

6   Ibid., p. 8.

7   Haki R. Madhubuti, Why L.A. Happened: Implications of the '92 Los Angeles Rebellion, pp. 32–33.

8   Ibid.

9   Ibid., p. 32.

10   Ibid., pp. 28–30.

11   Anna Kosof, The Civil Rights Movement and Its Legacy, p. 45.

12   Ibid.

13   Ibid., pp. 45–50.

14   Ibid., p. 41.

15   C. Eric Lincoln & Lawrence H. Mamiya, The Black Church in the African American Experience, p. 1.

16   Deburg, p. 237.

17   Ibid., p. 242.

18   Ibid.

19   Ibid., p. 134.

20   Ibid., p. 137.

21   Ibid., p. 140.

22   Ibid., pp. 140–141.

23   Ibid., pp. 145–147.

24   Ibid., p. 155.

25   Ibid., p. 157.

26   Ibid., p. 171.

27   Ibid., p. 172.

28   Ibid.

29   Ibid., p. 173.

30   Ibid., pp. 172–173.

31   Ibid., p. 179.

Footnotes- Part II
Chapter 4

1   Michael James, "Exodus: The Movement of My People," from a collection of poems, Love Is The Message, p. 1.

2   Dwight N. Hopkins, Introducing Black Theology of Liberation, p. 81.

3   "The Holocaust," Collier's Encyclopedia, Vol. 12, p. 197.

4   Ibid.

5   Ibid., p. 198.

6   Ibid.

7   "World War II," Collier's Encyclopedia, Vol. 23, p. 630.

8   Haki R. Madhubuti, Why L.A. Happened: Implications of the '92 Los Angeles Rebellion, p. 30.

9   Richard Hofrichter, Toxic Struggles: The Theory and Practices of Environmental Justice, p. 101.

10   Madhubuti, p. 52.

11   Ibid.

12   Hofrichter, pp. 59 & 70.

13   Ibid.

14   Ibid., p. 188.

15   Ibid., pp. 188–189.

16   Ibid., p. 63.

17   Ibid.

18   Ibid., p. 104.

19   Jean Dennis Cashman, African Americans and the Quest for Civil Rights, 1900-1990, p. 95.

20   Hofrichter, p. 212.

21   Fredrick K.C. Price, Race, Religion, and Racism, p. 161.

22   Ibid.

23   Ibid.

24   William L. Van Deburg, New Day in Babylon: The Black Power Movement and American Culture, 1965–1975, p. 240.

25   Dwight N. Hopkins, Shoes That Fit Our Feet, p. 195.

26   Ibid.

27   Ibid., 196.

Footnotes- The Final Word

1   Dwight N. Hopkins, Introducing Black Theology of Liberation, p. 37.

2   Dwight N. Hopkins, Shoes That Fit Our Feet: Sources for a Constructive Black Theology, p. 179.

3   Dwight N. Hopkins, Introducing Black Theology of Liberation, p. 198.

4   Ibid., p. 52.

5   Ibid., p. 37.

6   Ibid.

7   Fredrick K. C. Price, Race, Religion, and Racism, pp. 184–185.

8   Dwight N. Hopkins, Introducing Black Theology of Liberation, p. 51.

9   Ibid., p. 85.

10   Ibid., p. 48.

Black Theology, Black Power & Black Love
Bibliography

Breitman, George. *The Last Year of Malcolm X: The Evolution of a Revolution*. New York: Schocken Books, 1967.

Beker, Christiaan J. *Suffering and Hope*. Philadelphia: Fortress Press, 1987.

Boros, Ladislaus. *Pain and Providence*. Maryland: Christian Classics, 1966.

Bower, Anthony. *Cumus, the Rebel*. trans London: Penguin, 1962.

Cashman, Jean Dennis. *African Americans and the Quest For Civil Rights, 1900-1990*. New York: New York University Press, 1991.

Cone, James. *Martin & Malcolm & America: A Dream or a Nightmare*. New York: Orbis Books, 1991.

Cone, James. *For My People—Black Theology and the Black Church*. New York: Orbis Books, 1984.

Cone, James. *Black Theology & Black Power*. New York: Harper & Row Publishers, 1969.

Collier's Encyclopedia, Vol. 12. New York: MacMillan Educational Company. Division of MacMillan Inc., 1991.

Deburg, William L. Van. *New Day in Babylon: The Black Power Movement and American Culture, 1965-1975*. Chicago & London: University of Chicago Press, 1992.

Feider, Paul A. *The Christian Search for Meaning in Suffering*. Connecticut: Twenty-Third Publications, 1980.

Goldman, Peter. *The Death and Life of Malcolm X*. New York: Harper & Row Publishers, 1965.

Hopkins, Dwight. *Shoes That Fit Our Feet: Sources For a Constructive Black Theology*. New York: Orbis Books, 1993.

Hopkins, Dwight. *Introducing Black Theology of Liberation*. New York: Orbis Books, 1999.

James, Michael. *"Exodus The Movement of My People,"* From a collection of poems, *Love Is the Message*, 1993.

King, Martin Luther Jr. *Stride Toward Freedom: The Montgomery Story*. New York: Harper & Brothers Publishers, 1958.

Kosof, Anna. *The Civil Rights Movement and its Legacy*. New York: Franklin Watts, 1989.

Kreeft, Peter. *Making Sense out of Suffering*. Ann Arbor, Michigan: Servant Books, 1986.

Kunjufu, Jawanza. *Countering the Conspiracy to Destroy Black Boys*. Chicago: African American Images, 1994.

Lincoln, Eric C. and Mamiya, Lawrence H. *The Black Church in the African American Experience*. Durham & London: Duke University Press, 1990.

Madhubuti, Haki R. *Why L.A. Happened—Implications of the '92 Los Angeles Rebellion*. Chicago: Third World Press, 1993.

Price, Fredrick K.C. *Race, Religion, & Racism. Vol. One: A Bold Encounter With Division in the Church*. Los Angeles: Faith One Publishing, 1999.

Smith, Ervin. *The Ethics of Martin Luther King*, Jr. New York: E Mellen Press, 1981.

Union Seminary Quarterly Reviews, Vol XXIII No 4 (Summer 1968) *Toward a Political Hermeneutics of the Gospel*.

Walton, Hanes Jr. *The Political Philosophies of Martin Luther King, Jr.* Westport, Conn: Greenwood Publishing Corp, 1971.

Webster Dictionary (Basic School Edition) New York: Simon & Schuster, Inc. 1989.

X, Malcolm. (*edited by* Imam Benjamin Karim) *The End of White World Supremacy—Four Speeches by Malcolm X*. New York: Arcade Publishing, 1971.

Holy Bible (KJV—King James Version) Nashville: Thomas Nelson Publishers, 1970.

Organizations

Black Panther Party	Revolutionary Nationalist group formed in the late sixties
CORE	Congress of Racial Equality
MIA	Montgomery Improvement Association
NAACP	National Association for the Advancement of Colored People
RNA	Republic of New Africa
SCLC	Southern Christian Leadership Conference
SNCC	Student Nonviolent Coordinating Committee

African American Denominations

AME	African Methodist Episcopal
AMEZ	African Methodist Episcopal
CME	Christian Methodist Episcopal Zion
COGIC	Church of God in Christ
NBC	National Baptist Convention, USA Incorporated
PNBC	Progressive National Baptist Convention

NOTES

NOTES

NOTES

NOTES

NOTES

NOTES

NOTES

NOTES

NOTES

NOTES

NOTES

NOTES

NOTES